Thank God it's Monday

MINISTRY IN THE WORKPLACE

Mark Greene

SCRIPTURE UNION
130 CITY ROAD LONDON EC1V 2NJ

First published 1994

ISBN 0 86201 908 7

Cover design by Mark Carpenter Design Consultants.
Cover illustration by Chris Lloyd.
Book design by Tom Windsor.

British Library Cataloguing-in-Publication Data
A catalogue record for this book is available from the British Library.

Phototypeset by Intype, London.
Printed and bound in Great Britain by Cox and Wyman Ltd, Reading, Berkshire.

This book is dedicated with love and gratitude to the
memory of
Robert Martel
(1958–1994)
Secretary, colleague, example, friend
Who knew the secret
Philippians 4:11

Thanks particularly to

My colleagues at Ogilvy & Mather who put up
with me

The people of Trinity Baptist Church, New York, who
gave me so much

Bill Vallari and Jill Vellinger – examples and
encouragers at work

Glen Kleinknecht who first suggested I write this book

Alison Barr, my editor, who made it better

Dr Peter Cotterell who vetted it for error of all kinds

The students of London Bible College (probably the
finest theological college in the world and certainly
the best one in Northwood) who prayed for me to get
it finished

Katriina Greene, a minister in her workplace and my
wife, who made it possible for me to get it finished

Contents

First thoughts

There are a lot of stories in this book.

They're all true.

Some of them are about success. Some of them are about abject failure. They're all about God at work. Indeed, there were days when God seemed to be doing so many things that I hardly had time to record them all in my diary. Amazing, exhilarating times they were.

As I look back on all that happened, what hits me again and again is a sense of wonder – our God cares, our God is at work, our God uses us with all our clumsiness and mixed motives and lack of knowledge. Our God does great things.

I have told these stories not to suggest that God will act in the same way in your workplace – may he move in even greater ways – but simply to illustrate that he is at work – at work. That the God who brought water from the rock, who changed water into wine, who raised Lazarus from the dead, does great things today. Indeed, as I look back I'm filled with wonder at his power, timing, sense of humour, grace and ability to use even the most unpromising circumstances for his ends. It was a joyous privilege to experience that. I wish you that joy.

1

Into the lion's den
Or the 'no go' zone

'Surely the Lord is in this place, and I was not aware of it.'

Genesis 28:16

• SNAPSHOTS •

I am a Jewish Christian and it is the second night of Passover. A group of us are going to celebrate it together in my flat. One of the people coming has prepared a chicken. She brings it to work and we decide to put it in the fridge in my boss's office. My boss is out that week but David Ogilvy, the man who founded the company I work for and the world's greatest living adman, is visiting and using the office off and on.

I have wanted to talk to him about God. I have prayed for an opportunity to talk to him about God but so far I haven't found either the courage or the opportunity. Or the courage to try to create the opportunity. I am very junior and he is the founder of the world's fourth largest advertising agency.

At four o'clock that afternoon, I realise it is time to collect the chicken and go and prepare the Passover. I wander round to my boss's office. David Ogilvy is in there talking on the phone. I wait a couple of minutes. The talking stops.

He is in there. And he has my chicken.

I am out here. And I have six people coming for supper.

It's getting late.

How should I introduce myself to the founder of the fourth largest advertising agency in the world? Will I be fired for trying to convert the founder? What should I say to the world's greatest living adman? Perhaps, 'Hello, I've come to collect my chicken.' And I realise that God is using this dead, half-roasted chicken to force me into David Ogilvy's presence. And I am sure that God who knows both my lack of courage and my taste for bad puns has had a lot of fun choosing a 'chicken' as the thing that forces me to overcome my cowardice. I knock. I walk into the lion's den. All my clever lines desert me. The greatest living adman looks up and says: 'Come in, sit down, who are you?' We talk for an hour or so – and somehow the conversation turns quickly and easily to God.

God at work.

And I wasn't fired.

We are in a bar having a farewell drink for one of the team. I'm talking to Susan. We've been working together for about a year and we get round to C S Lewis. Barbara (or at least that's what we'll call her) is with us. She's Jewish, bright and fun.

'Is that the same C S Lewis who wrote the Narnia Chronicles?'

'Yes.'

'I love those books. He's my hero. I didn't know he was a Christian.'

'Oh, yes and there's Christian allegory in the books. Aslan is Jesus . . .'

'Yeah, but Aslan comes back to life . . .'

God at work. The Christian at work.

It's two o'clock in the afternoon.

He is not having a very wonderful day.

An angel comes and leaves a chocolate on his desk.

The Christian at work.

Three aspects of ministry in the workplace.

David Ogilvy and the opportunities God gives us when we step outside our circle of confidence.

Barbara and C S Lewis – the opportunities God gives us when we spend time with people outside the workplace.

A chocolate on the desk – the opportunities God gives us to express love and kindness to those we work with in our everyday routine.

The workplace is God's place, and his place is just as much there as in the church prayer meeting. The workplace is a place of opportunity – a place to express the compassion of the gospel in word and deed, to challenge non-biblical thinking and practice, to grow in faith and character and love.

God at work in us.

God at work through us.

God at work in those we work with.

GOD'S PLACE

There are few subjects I feel are more neglected, few issues that excite me more, few areas of ministry that could do more to transform the nature of society than witness at work. There are few things that could do more to invigorate and release us as Christians than to be equipped for ministry in the place where many of us spend sixty to seventy percent of our waking lives . . .

It is putting workplace ministry on the agenda that I am most concerned about. I am concerned about it because I am concerned about people – that all may be saved. And I am concerned about society – that the meat may be salted and the rot stopped.

The Church today is engaged in a Decade of Evangelism. The Church is doing its research and concluding that the people on the fringe of today's churches are fewer and fewer, that the people who know even the basics of Christian claims are fewer and fewer, that the Church must go out to the people on the fringe and the people beyond the fringe and win them there. That the Church must develop services for them that are in their language, not ours.

Indeed.

But where in all this grand strategy have we heard anyone whisper – the workplace?

We are encouraged to develop relationships with our neighbours. Quite right. We are encouraged to develop relationships with non-Christian friends. Quite right. But how much time do you spend with even your best friend in a month? Two hours, three hours, four hours. Ten hours?

We are encouraged to bring people to guest services. We are encouraged to sing carols outside Tesco's or to get involved in putting on a concert to which we will invite our non-Christian friends. All good things. But are we encouraged to witness at work?

And the overwhelming answer in most cases is 'no'. Seventy five percent of the people I have surveyed have never been asked by their minister about their ministry in their workplace.

Peanuts and puddles

Are we working at the margins and forgetting the centre? Playing with peanuts and aperitifs when there's a main course to get stuck into? Sending Christians out into the highways and byways when the room is full of people? Struggling to develop relationships with the strangers next door when our neighbour is just a desk away?

This is a great tragedy. Because Christians in work spend more time in the workplace than any other place. The workplace is day in day out the one place where non-Christians can see the difference that being a Christian makes – the one place Christian and non-Christian face the same stresses, may have the same boss, may be rebuked for similar failures, praised for similar successes, are subject to the same structural dynamics, to the same corporate culture, the same food, the same gossip . . .

There are very few places where a non-Christian could and should see the difference that Christ makes in a life so clearly as in working with someone thirty, forty, sixty hours a week.

We are being called on to look for common ground with non-Christians when, *in the workplace*, we already share it.

We are being exhorted to build bridges when, *in the workplace*, the bridges are already built and have been crossed.

We are exhorted to go and develop relationships with people but, *in the workplace*, the relationships already exist. We are encouraged to go out and fish in pools and puddles when we're sitting on a lake full of fish.

The unavoidable witness

Importantly, in the workplace the witness comes in a form that cannot be tuned out like a radio programme, zapped like a TV broadcast, thrown away like a tract or turned down like the invitation to a concert. The non-Christian can tune out almost every form of the gospel but he cannot, short of murder or Machiaevellian office politics tune out the spectacle of the Christian living in the power of the Spirit day by day, hour by hour, crisis by crisis.

Furthermore the workplace is the one place where Christians can't avoid contact with non-Christians. In every other area we can schedule non-Christians out – making friends mainly with Christians, ministering in a housegroup, serving on a church committee, going to the church prayer meeting, attending church on Sunday. And so on. The workplace is the one place where adult Christians are forced to meet non-Christians. The one place where Christian and non-Christian have to relate to one another.

That's why it is critical for evangelism.

If the Church is looking for people who are beyond the fringe it will find many of them in the same workplaces as their members.

If the Church is looking to stop the rot it will find that the rot is in many of the companies for which its members work – where there are poor payment practices, the abuse of smaller suppliers, unjust appraisal systems, racist, sexist hiring policies, bribery, corruption, Dirty Tricks campaigns, competitiveness which is not a spur to excellence but a goad to deceit. As John Stott put it, you can't blame the meat for going rotten, blame the salt . . .

But for most Christians work is not a mission field.

And work is not a primary or even a secondary context for ministry.

And work is not the place to challenge non-Christian worldviews and management practices.

Why not?

Pressure from society?

There are pressures from society. Society encourages us to believe that our faith is private and has no place in the working world. And indeed the working world operates on an atheistic basis. God, it believes, does not show up on the balance sheet. What we do in our own time is up to us but there's no place for biblical ethics and claims about truth on the factory floor or in the board meeting.

This anti-Christian prejudice leads to fear of not fitting in, fear of not getting promoted, fear of losing my job. If I do speak out for my faith, if I refuse to tap into a rival airline's computers, will I still be getting a paycheque next month? Real fears with plenty of foundation in experience.

The church against evangelism?

However, in many cases the major source of pressure against witness at work comes from the local church. Most churches are in fact, if not by conviction, primarily focused on building up their own local congregation.

The minister's concerns relate to his neighbourhood and he rightly wants his church community to be engaged in evangelism. As a result the church develops programmes which relate to the concerns of people in the immediate area. In turn, the minister mobilises resources behind this neighbourhood effort.

However, for the most part church programmes encourage us to relate to cold contacts, people we don't know that well, people we haven't met until we stand outside Tesco's or knock on their doors, people who are our neighbours but who, for the most part, only want a semi-detached kind of relationship with those who live close by. Church evangelism is, if you like, a cold contact farm.

Today, however, many people's primary relationships are not in their neighbourhood. Changes in work and transport patterns mean that the people we spend most time with often do not live near the church.

Many of our warm contacts are at work.

If we're looking for contacts then this may well be the place to begin. After all the average person probably meets, talks to, eats with, writes to, works with over a hundred people a week.

Warm contacts.

The forgotten kingdom

The local church, however, may well be mobilised 'to do church' in a particular neighbourhood, rather than to equip its people to build the kingdom wherever God has placed its members. And this may be further reflected in the way church members are encouraged.

If you go to the deacons' meeting you are affirmed by your fellow Christians, by the leadership of the church. If you stay on at the office to go out for a drink with a co-worker you are not. In other words there is no mechanism for affirmation of the working person – except in crisis. Indeed, fifty percent of the Christians I have surveyed have never heard a single sermon on work. That is, they have never had any biblical teaching on the area of life that is meant to occupy them six days a week.

For what ministry then are our ministers equipping their flocks? Probably for the ministries of the local church. For the ministries which revolve around the minister's skills and gifts. In other words, are our leaders inadvertently equipping us to support their ministry rather than equipping us to do the work of *ours*?

Is your minister looking to see how your gifts can fit into the church's needs? Or is he asking how God can use you to further the work of the kingdom? Is he asking: where else, apart from in this church, has God placed you? To what ministry are you called? Where is God calling you to exercise your gifts? If my research is anything to go by, I suspect not.

There is a significant danger that church evangelistic strategies will inadvertently be designed around getting people into church to hear the minister when the more important issue is getting people into the kingdom by hearing the word of God. Of course, our leaders are not deliberately seeking to inhibit our ministry or build their own. Work has simply become unimportant on all our spiritual agendas.

If you're a good Bible study leader, do you think to yourself: 'I'd like to take on a housegroup?' Or do you think: 'You know, I'm quite good at leading Bible studies. Maybe I should start one at work.' And it's a rare thing indeed for someone to come up and ask you: 'How's your witness at work? What particular issues are you facing at work?'

This is also reflected in preaching and teaching.

As I've mentioned, over fifty percent of Christians I have surveyed have never heard a sermon on work. Over seventy percent have never been taught a theology of work. Which is even more extraordinary when you think that probably ninety five percent of Christians have heard sermons on Genesis 1–3 which, as we'll see later, is no bad place to start looking for a theology of work. Under twenty five percent have ever been asked by their minister about their witness at work. Whereas I suspect that almost everyone who's been in a church for more than a year has been encouraged to get involved with one of the church's ministries. Finally, only twenty six percent have ever been asked by their minister to consider developing a ministry in the workplace. Sobering statistics. The reality of the overall situation is probably far worse since this research was conducted among highly motivated groups.

An unholy hierarchy
This overall marginalisation of work is further reflected in a belief within the Church which goes something like this:

> All Christians
> are born
> equal
> but
> 'full-time'
> Christians
> are more equal
> than others.

In turn, there is an unspoken hierarchy that goes something like this:

> Pastor
> Overseas Missionary
> Full-time Christian Worker
> Tentmaker (*as long as it's abroad*)
> Elder
> Deacon
> Poor Christian

Christian
Rich Christian
Former Advertising Executives

The fact is that we have, to a very large extent, completely lost the sense that God might call someone to a secular job, or indeed, to unpaid work in the home, and that either of these may be just as strategic in his economy as pastoring a church. We no longer have a theology of vocation.

Indeed, it is very easy for students training in theological institutions to be apologetic or defensive if they feel that God is calling them into secular work. As if it's second best. Others may feel pressured into going into full-time Christian work by the expectations of church and supporters: 'We haven't sent you to Bible College just so you can go back into the oil business.'

And that, I believe, reflects the fact that we may not really believe 2 Timothy 3:16–17:

> All Scripture is God-breathed and is useful for teaching, rebuking, correcting and training in righteousness that the person of God may be equipped for *every* good work.

For every good work. But when someone leaves school or university or Bible College and takes a job at Sainsbury's, will the church pray specifically for the ministry to which God has set them apart?

It is indeed fine to study the Bible in order to use our secular jobs as a platform for evangelism and ministry in Saudi Arabia, but at Kodak in Harrow? The irony is that Kodak may be an unreached people group every bit as needy as the Saudis, or the Rendille in Kenya. Or the Kalahari bushpeople. Indeed, when I started my last secular job I was, as far as I knew, the only Christian in that workplace. One in a thousand. 0.1% of the population. A missionary need to rival that of Tunisia, Iran, Turkey. And, it might be added, a missionary enterprise that would need no funds from the church since it would be funded entirely by my employers.

In fact, one might argue that Christians need a good theological education even more to work in a secular organisation than to work in a church. Precisely because the worldview of the secular organisation may be so fundamentally opposed to Christianity that the daily challenge of working through the variety of issues and problems may take a great deal of discernment. Particularly since you may well be the only Christian in that company. Think for a moment of the difficult ethical decisions involved in any job in healthcare. Ask a Christian teacher or lawyer about the challenges they face. Talk to someone on the factory floor about communicating the gospel to their workmates. Writing a sermon is comparatively safe. At least there's a whole host of people to tell you when you've got it wrong.

So, in my view the Church does not believe 2 Timothy 3:16–17 or there would be a flood of young people aged 18–23 taking a year or two at Bible colleges before or after going to college or starting work. And there aren't many. And there would be a number of Bible colleges offering courses and options specifically designed for people going into secular work. And there aren't many.

Believe it or not?
There are several other things we don't really believe:
• All vocations are equal and so-called 'secular' work is a vocation.
• Many of our biblical heroes were in fact workers.

The Israelite midwives – who, struggling for biblical medical ethics, boldly defied Pharoah's command to kill all male babies; Naaman's strategically placed servant girl, who courageously told her pagan master that healing was to be found in a foreign land; Lydia the merchant; Joseph, the chancellor; Daniel, the imperial advisor, Nehemiah, the security agent – people like these are often perceived and presented as 'spiritual' giants, children's heroes, rather than as ordinary women and men working out their faith in their workplaces.

Here are some other things we don't really believe:

• All work needs to be done in line with the word of God and to his glory.

• God is interested in every part of our lives.

• Secular work can be a privilege and a joy.

• Proverbs is an important book of the Bible. If we believed that, there would be a lot more teaching from Proverbs. And then we would hear a lot more about work.

In sum, there is a great danger that we as Christians will accept the division that non-believers make between the public world of work and the private world of faith, that we will seek to limit God's activities to non-working hours.

But does God save people in the workplace?

Yes.

Does God heal in the workplace?

Well, yes, in my experience he does.

Does God love justice and mercy in the workplace?

Of course.

Is God's work limited in any significant way by the demands and disciplines of the workplace?

Surely not.

The guilt-edged Christian

The impact on Christians of effectively robbing their work of spiritual and ministry value is to produce a sense of guilt. The working Christian comes home at the end of a fifty hour week and thinks: 'I haven't done any evangelism. I haven't done any ministry. I'm not serving God. I must make time outside work to do all these things otherwise I'm not leading an obedient Christian life.' So perhaps the person does get involved in neighbourhood evangelism or accepts the invitation to serve on the diaconate and tries to squeeze a hundred commitments into a seven day week. And the result of that can simply be exhaustion and discouragement. Exhaustion because too much is being attempted; discouragement because perhaps there isn't much to show for a lot of extra effort. And because there is this sneaking suspicion that the thing we spend thirty, forty, fifty hours a week doing is of no intrinsic value to God – whether it's typing letters, looking after children, fixing cars or fixing people. God's not interested in it. After all my minister isn't and my Christian friends aren't, so surely it follows that *he* isn't.

And that unspoken but real belief stems not only from lack of encouragement but also from the failure to apply biblical truths about identity, about God's love, about the ministry of the Spirit to our working lives.

The absentee Spirit?

God doesn't change when we walk into work.

But maybe we do.

The Holy Spirit doesn't suddenly realise he's in an office or a factory and say, 'I'm off now. See you later at the prayer meeting.'

The Holy Spirit, the spirit of mission doesn't say: 'Well, here we are in the office. Forget the evangelism bit, forget the gifts bit, I'm just into the fruits bit now. Let's just concentrate on Galatians 5, on love, joy, peace, patience, kindness, goodness, faithfulness, gentleness and self-control from eight to six, and we'll get back to drawing people into relationship with Christ later on this evening.'

This book is about living an integrated Christian life at work as well as outside work. It is about God at work in our workplace as well as outside it. It is about living in the confidence of God's resources at work as well as outside work. It is about the fact that God's place is always first wherever we are, whatever we do, whoever we work for.

Of course, we cannot all do all things. God doesn't call all working Christians to focus their ministry on the workplace. But I do long to see Christians released into ministry where they are.

I long to see Christians go out expectantly to work and come home exhilarated – like Jesus at the well, so empowered and thrilled by his ministry to the Samaritan woman that though his disciples urged him to eat something he said:

> 'I have food to eat that you know nothing about
> . . . My food . . . is to do the will of him who sent
> me and to finish his work. Do you not say, "Four
> months more and then the harvest"? I tell you,
> open your eyes and look at the fields! They are
> ripe for harvest.'
>
> *John 4:34–35*

For many, many Christians the workplace is, I believe, a harvest field. This book is about working there.

EPILOGUE

MODELS FOR OUR TIME
On the Buses
Or a working heroine is something to be

Penny has been on the buses for seven years.

She's a warm, down-to-earth, no-nonsense sort of lady. It's not an easy job: trying to soothe stroppy, frozen-footed, frustrated passengers who've waited forty five minutes in the rain for the one that didn't come; trying to treat everyone who asks for a ticket as a human being, as somebody in God's plan; trying to go by the rules and not let the pensioners onto the bus before nine just because 'all the other drivers do'; trying to chat to her regulars, some of whom are just plain lonely and come out for a ride into town for the company. Trying and sometimes blowing it. Being herself and, as she puts it, trusting that through it all God will use her somehow.

It's a tough place to work.

Lots of affairs, lots of divorce, lots of gossip. 'Pen', as they call her, tries not to get involved. Sometimes she says, 'I don't want to hear about it.' Sometimes she simply withdraws from the scene. People miss her. She responds: 'I don't want to spend my free time cooped up in an office talking about everyone's ins and outs.' But when the chips are down it's often Pen people tell things to. After all, they can be sure she's not going to sit in an office blabbing it to the world. Similarly, it's often others who ask her questions about Jesus. They just come to her. She laughs with a mixture of joy and disbelief that God uses her in this way. 'I feel unworthy of it really.'

Occasionally the mockery of Christ is sharp. One man around Easter time, stretched out his arms to form a cross and said: 'Not my idea of a fun way to spend Easter.' But Pen isn't judgemental and doesn't expect people who don't know God to live by his rules. People respect her. She's not one to stop anyone's mouth but on occasion her colleagues, sensing that a particularly rich anecdote is about to turn the air blue, curb it with the phrase, 'Not while Pen's here.' And of course from time to time she's mocked for being a bit 'old-fashioned' – 'have another drink', 'get a man' kind of stuff. Every worldview has its evangelists. And then folk are mildly shocked to discover that she'll have a lager from time to time and that she's reading a book about a group of contract killers going after five SAS men. And murdering four of them.

Sometimes it saddens her that some people put her in a box. 'We Christians are obviously a strange breed to them. And sometimes I feel like a bit of an alien.'

She pauses.

'But that, I suppose, is what we are.'

Christian by design
Or a working hero is something to be

Brett is a graphic designer. Thirty three and stopped counting. He started out on his own, working freelance, taking his work round to show people. Getting rejected. Getting accepted. Today he's one of the directors of a smallish design and printing company that's survived the recession. Just. He works hard and long. Often for some of the weekend. He's well off but doesn't have lots left over for weekend trips to San Moritz. He's married to Page and they have four children, and a three bedroom semi that's full of love and life and stuff and lots of people.

Brett is a Christian. He's also pretty determined and gets up at around five to spend time with God. Up to an hour – depending on when the kids explode into life. On the way to work he listens to the music that's out there – REM, Grant Lee Buffalo, Van Morrison, whatever, and from time to time a music scripture memory tape. In the middle of the day he does weights. And looks like it. I'm always polite to Brett.

He's been to Bible College and has a good degree in theology. He's putting it to use at work, in the way he does it, in the way he treats his clients, in the way he helps his people when they've got a problem. And he's putting it to work in his family and in running one of his church's youth groups – forty to fifty teenagers, lots of pizza, houseparties, summer outreach cafes in the local High Street and serious, well thought-out, no-holds-barred Bible studies that give the lie to the idea that all you can give teenagers is spiritual jelly and ice cream.

Now *there's* a model for our time.

After all, more teenagers are likely to end up as family people with secular jobs than as full-time ministers in a church.

He's not the only model, of course, but even if the Bretts of this world are largely unsung heroes, Paul, the great missionary, would probably have approved. He, after all, spent a fair amount of time making tents for a living.

2

Another day, another dime?
Or a short theology of work

'The Christian community has a specific task . . . to regain the lost sense of work as a divine calling.'

Emil Brunner

'Nothing is work unless you would rather be doing something else.'

William James

THE WORKER GOD

In the beginning God.

Then he started work.

The Bible describes creation as the work of God – six days he worked. And on the seventh he rested from all the work that he had done. God is a worker. And work was something he chose to do. Part of his plan. Consistent with his holy nature. And as he considered his work at its various stages he pronounced it good – good after he made light, good after the third day and the fourth and the fifth. And very good as he considered all that he had done.

God's work is obviously distinguished from our work by the fact that he is all-powerful and his work is perfect, but his work of creation did involve many functions we think of as work:

- He makes things – as a craftsman might.
- He categorises and names things – as a zoologist might.
- He carries out his work in a clearly planned order – not all at once it seems – the water and sky must wait three days for the fish and the birds, the land three days for the animals.
- He examines the quality of his work at every stage – as a fine artist or a responsible manufacturer might.

• He assigns clearly defined functions to the components of creation – as a good engineer might – the
greater light to govern the day and the lesser light to
govern the night.

• He assigns a clearly defined role for humanity and
provides the resources to fulfil that role – as a good
manager might.

Furthermore, God's work reflects who he is. He
creates humanity in his own image. We may not have
his logo on us but all humanity bears his stamp, as
perhaps we would like our work to do. A letter
immaculately typed. A component faultlessly tooled.
Something we want to be associated with.

Finally, God takes pleasure in his work – as perhaps
we all do when a job is well done. When he's finished,
he sees that it is 'very good'.

So the Bible introduces us to God as the creator and
describes his involvement in creation as his work. Work
that he does voluntarily, with pleasure and satisfaction.

Work before the Fall
Furthermore, God gives humanity work to do.
Humanity is designed for work, the work of subduing
the earth and ruling over the animal world. And that
work is clearly given as a blessing:

> God blessed them and said to them, 'Be fruitful
> and increase in number, fill the earth and subdue
> it. Rule over the fish of the sea and the birds of
> the air and over every living creature that moves
> on the ground.'

And more specifically in chapter 2:15:

> God took the man and put him in the Garden of
> Eden to work it and take care of it.'

It is interesting to note that God gives two commands – not just to work the garden but also to take care of it. There is in this command the human obligation to preserve the earth, not simply to exploit it for our own ends. Bulldozing Brazilian rainforests, working the soil to exhaustion for three years and then leaving it as a wasteland is not an option.

The main point for our purposes is to note that work is not a consequence of the Fall but part of the original plan. We were always meant to work. And work was intended as a source of satisfaction and pleasure.

After the Fall
When humanity rebelled against God the character of work was changed. It would never be so easy again:

> 'By the sweat of your brow
> you will eat of your food . . .'
>
> *Genesis 3:19*

Nevertheless, this did not change the command to rule over the earth and subdue it. It did not change the command to work, nor the essential value of work. Indeed, God does not simply banish Adam from Eden he banishes him *and* tells him 'to work the ground from which he had been taken' (Genesis 3:23). And although there will be toil this does not mean that there will not also be satisfaction in work. God said that the pain women bear in childbirth would increase but that does not mean there is no joy in having children. All creation was marred by Adam's sin but the earth is still beautiful and the psalmist can still write with wonder that 'The heavens declare the glory of God; the skies proclaim the work of his hands' (Psalm 19:1). There is punishment but also grace. The command to work is maintained even if the way that the work is done is radically changed.

The connection between God as worker and humanity as workers is further stressed by the call to imitate God in the shape of the working week – God works six days and then rests on the seventh, at least from the work of creation. Humanity is to do the same. This suggests that one way in which we reflect the image of God is in our work. And that work, in Genesis at least, is directly connected to looking after what he has created.

The affirmation of work pervades Scripture.

Even Ecclesiastes, a book not noted for its optimism, affirms work:

> Then I realised that it is good and proper for a man to eat and drink, and to find satisfaction in his toilsome labour under the sun during the few days of life God has given him – for this is his lot.

Ecclesiastes 5:18

He goes on to say that to be happy in one's work is 'a gift of God' and that through work God keeps a person occupied with 'gladness of heart'. Ecclesiastes is not, however, under any illusions. He still describes work as 'toilsome labour under the sun'. So the fact that there can be satisfaction in work is not to say that work is always pleasurable, or that periods of frustration and boredom at work are signs of divine displeasure, but it is to state that work *is* a legitimate source of satisfaction and a divinely ordained part of the human condition.

Work then is not man's idea. It is God's. Work is not an intermission from the main action, something we do so that we can then do other things, it is an integral part of the main action, an intrinsic part of our walk with God.

The limits of work

Nevertheless, the Old Testament as a whole put limits on the significance of work. Ecclesiastes himself recognises that *in itself* work does not have ultimate value:

> 'My heart took delight in all my work,
> and this was the reward for all my labour.
> Yet when I surveyed all that my hands had done
> and what I had toiled to achieve,
> everything was meaningless, a
> chasing after the wind . . .'

Ecclesiastes 2:10–11

If we look for our significance in our work we will come away with empty hearts. Our significance lies in our relationship with the Creator of work.

Similarly Exodus and Deuteronomy put work in perspective and set clear limits to the amount of time we spend working – six days. The seventh was to be a Sabbath – a rest day. And the command not to work on that day finds expression throughout the Old Testament. Several reasons are given for the command:
– so we can acknowledge God as Creator honouring his designation of the Sabbath as a blessed and holy day
– so we can rest
– so we can allow others to rest as a way of preventing their exploitation.

Stop in the name of God

God is the Lord of time and time is a gift of God to us. On the seventh day he called the Israelites to set aside their time to him. Today we need to set aside the frantic drive to put every day, every minute to profitable use, to meet our agenda and slake our thirst for the security we think we can find in constant activity. Time is what many of us feel we don't have enough of – so there is always the temptation to break the rhythm of work and rest that God lays down.

The command to rest applied not only to the Israelites but also to foreigners who worked for them. Deuteronomy 5:15 reinforces the command to give slaves the day off by reminding the people of their experience of tyrannical slavery in Egypt. The people of God must not exercise power in a similar way. Limits are set on material gain – the people of God are to keep the Sabbath even when the ploughing and the harvesting is being done. In other words even when the time to accomplish the work is limited:

> '... on the seventh day you shall rest; even during the ploughing season and harvest you must rest.'
>
> *Exodus 34:21*

Don't work on the Sabbath – even though the seeds may be planted too late, the rain may come and the harvest may go rotten. Humanity needs to recognise God as the provider, to put him before greed, to set aside anxiety and put limits on gainful labour. There is no room for the materialism that drives people to a seven day week. Nor is there room for the workaholism that turns work into an idol that determines the entire shape of one's life. That pushes God out and puts work in first place.

In Old Testament thought the Sabbath becomes a crucial indicator of fidelity to the God of Israel. In Isaiah 56 the Lord promises his blessing on those who maintain justice and do what is right, who stop their hands from doing evil and keep the Sabbath without desecrating it. Keeping the Sabbath is the only specific mentioned amongst a number or general exhortations to live in line with God's character. Similarly, God promises a memorial and a name to the eunuchs 'who keep my Sabbaths, who choose what pleases me and hold fast to my covenant . . .' (Isaiah 56:4) Again in verse 6 God promises his blessing on foreigners, based on their overall commitment and love for God *and* the keeping of the Sabbath.

The New Testament clarifies the teaching in one vitally important way. The key text is Mark 2:27:

> 'The Sabbath was made for humankind, not humankind for the Sabbath.'
>
> *New Revised Standard Version*

In other words the Sabbath is there for our benefit. It is intended as a blessing not a means of preventing rest and refreshment. That said, the New Testament releases us from the *command* to dedicate one day to God. The new life in Christ is life in the spirit so there is the freedom to discern prayerfully how to apply the principle of rest, of giving God time, of not worshipping work, of setting limits on the time we spend working for money. Nevertheless, the principles should in my view be applied. We may be released from the mandate to take a particular day off but we are surely unwise to ignore the principles the Creator has laid down for our benefit.

Work as worship

The New Testament, like the Old, affirms the value of work. Jesus was a carpenter by trade. Manual labour is a dignified occupation not just for the son of Joseph but for the Son of God. Work is both necessary and good. God does not take the Christian out of the world, rather he transforms all aspects of life in the world. Including work. In line with this Paul calls on Christians to do their work for God. Work becomes one of the ways humanity serves God. It becomes a component of our worship. Interestingly, Hebrew uses the same word for 'worship' as for 'work' – *avodah*. The English word 'service' perhaps comes closest to capturing both meanings. Work, then, is worship. It's for God and, as we shall see later, that has radical implications for our attitude to the quality of our performance.

What is work?
In our age work has increasingly been defined in economic terms – work is what you are paid to do. You're not working if you're not earning a wage. And you have less status if you are not working. This applies not just to the unemployed but to people like housewives and househusbands who don't receive a wage for their efforts. Indeed, one of the most tragic cries of Western culture is: 'Oh, I'm just a housewife'. This seems to reflect many women's feeling that their work is valueless and of no possible interest to anyone. Why? Because it's not paid? Or because it is repetitive? Because it involves a lot of tasks that are *perceived* as not requiring a great deal of skill? However, forty years ago being a 'homemaker' was a highly respected and valued form of work. The devaluation of the role highlights the need to be wary of definitions of work that relate to a particular culture.

The Bible resists a definition of work that relates merely to earning a wage. Making beds and cleaning floors is work not only when it's done by a paid auxiliary in a hospital, it is work when it's done by a housewife or a househusband. Plumbing in a washing machine is work not just when it's done by a professional plumber, it's work when mum does it on Saturday after a long week in the sales office.

So definitions of what constitutes rest may vary from person to person.

It might mean, for example, that a housewife (or househusband) should be relieved of the cooking one day a week. It is after all what she does every day. Cooking is part of her contribution to the economic process, allowing her partner to leave the home to earn money. Should she 'cease' from this task? One characteristic of the Sabbath does seem to be a change in the nature of activity from the other six days – stopping what one does most of the time. Indeed, the Hebrew word for Sabbath means to stop or cease. So work might be defined as the activities you are principally engaged in during the week, whether in or out of the home, 'employed' or 'unemployed'.

Working for ourselves, working for others
Work certainly includes what we do to provide for ourselves and those we are responsible for:

> If anyone does not provide for his relatives, and especially for his immediate family, he has denied the faith and is worse than an unbeliever.
> *1 Timothy 5:8*

This is a remarkably strong statement and could easily lead to false guilt, particularly for those who are unemployed through no fault of their own. Paul, however, was writing for a community where work was available. That said, his statement reveals how important it is to create a society where it is possible for people to provide for their own and their family's material needs. Denying someone the ability to provide for his or her own family denies that person a fundamental form of human expression.

Work includes any activity that contributes to provision – cooking, washing, food shopping, car maintenance – as well as those activities that generate money directly.

The purposes of work, however, extend beyond simple material provision for ourselves and our immediate family:

• We work so that we can give to those who don't have – note Paul's remarkable statement about the necessity for reformed thieves to work so that they can give to those in need (Ephesians 4:28).

• We work to serve others, to improve life for the community as a whole – the baker baking bread, the car maker making cars, the writer writing, the 'housespouse' teaching his child to walk, the nurse caring for a patient – all contribute to the quality of community life.

• We work to develop gifts and skills, to express ourselves through the tasks we do, to gain the satisfaction of a job well done, to rejoice in our God-given abilities.

Provision, service, personal development – all good reasons to work but none of them good reasons to turn work into an idol, to sacrifice our friends and families at its all-consuming altar, to say that extra work is being done for the good of the family when in fact the family is being destroyed by the workaholism of absentee parents. God created human beings for relationship with him and with one another. And he created work as a blessing for us, as a means of provision and mutual service. He did not create us to be slaves of work. Nevertheless, in a society where some people seem to have too much work to do and others have none to do at all, in a society where many live in fear of unemployment and many others live in despair of ever finding paid work, keeping work in godly perspective is no easy job.

3

Winning away
Or how to avoid a split personality

*'I can do everything through him who gives
me strength.'*
The Apostle Paul, Philippians 4:13

WINNING AWAY

In most sports it's harder to win away from home. The rules don't change, you don't change, the opposition doesn't change but the ground changes and there's a psychological disadvantage in playing in front of predominantly hostile supporters.

We know that our God's character does not change. We know that our God is love. But are we convinced that his love is as much directed to the people at ICI as the people at St Michael's? As much concerned for Welsh miners as Papuan tribesmen? God loves people constantly, all day and all night. Weekdays and Sundays. He loves them when they're in the factory and when they're not in the factory. God is at work at work. His identity does not change. He is in the business of completing his purposes in us and through us. And in and through the people around us. Home and away. At home. At work.

The Bible tells us that Jesus Christ is the same yesterday, today and forever. He died to give us abundant life. And this abundant life is ours not only when we are at home, or in Bible studies, or in church services but in our life as a secretary or a nurse or a mechanic or a stockbroker. There is no division. If the Christian life doesn't work nine to five then maybe it's no more than a nice leisure activity like aerobics, golf or crocheting.

God's identity does not change after nine.

And our identity does not change either.

Prince or pauper?

You may think that you are a computer programmer, a waitress, an editor, an engineer, a cook. . . You are also something very grand. You are a child of God (John 1:12). A child of the king. And therefore a prince or princess. This idea has always rather appealed to me, especially since my idea of a prince is so firmly rooted in historical fables – a noble, courageous, compassionate paragon of virtue, with a flowing red velvet cape and a black stallion. Irresistible. Wishful thinking on my part, I'm afraid. Nevertheless, we are royalty. It may not feel that way. In fact, it may feel the opposite – we may feel abused, unappreciated, a dispensable cog in a heartless machine – but our essential identity in Christ is not changed by how people treat us. Christ is in us:

> Therefore, if anyone is in Christ he is a new creation; the old has gone, the new has come!
>
> *2 Corinthians 5:17*

We are a new creation and Christ *is* in us. The Christian's identity does not change according to his circumstances. We don't become secularised, despiritualised, unholy when we are in the workplace. We are still new creatures, still a royal priesthood, still heirs of marvelous promises, still called to holiness, still promised the power to resist temptation, still promised the fruits of the Spirit. Certainly we may have a different role at work but that does not make us different people. Nevertheless, to be consistent, we need to call on God's help to live according to our true identity, whatever the pressure. Easier written than done, but God has provided the resources.

We go to work with God's authority and in his power. We go to work as his ambassadors with his message. We need to have confidence in those resources and in that message.

> 'For we are ambassadors for Christ, God making his appeal through us.'
>
> *2 Corinthians 5:20*

Today probably more than ninety five percent of British people don't know Jesus in a personal way – God makes his appeal through us.

Today many of our major institutions are strongholds of secular humanist thought. Strongholds that can be taken captive to obey Christ:

> The weapons we fight with are not the weapons of the world. On the contrary, they have divine power to demolish strongholds. We demolish arguments and every pretension that sets itself up against the knowledge of God, and we take captive every thought to make it obedient to Christ.
>
> *2 Corinthians 10:4–5*

This vision of strong Christian corporate influence may seem like a fantasy in the pressure and hurly burly of the every day, but we do need to be careful before we dismiss it. After all, who would have thought that a servant of the living God would become a pagan empire's chief administrator? That's what happened to Daniel, who began his career as just one of a group of talented Israelite youths deported to Babylon and, without ever compromising his faith, was subsequently promoted to head of the civil service. The whole empire may not in Daniel's time have bowed down to the God of Israel. But it was run in a way that reflected Daniel's reliance on the wisdom of the words and ways of the God of Abraham, Isaac and Jacob . . . wisdom that caused Darius, his boss, to seek to promote him to chief administrator of the entire empire and then, after the incident in the lions' den, to protect the religious rights of the Jewish people:

> 'I issue a decree that in every part of my kingdom people must fear and reverence the God of Daniel.'
>
> *Daniel 6:26*

The God of Daniel is our God. As Darius put it:

> 'For he is the living God
> and he endures for ever,
> his kingdom will not be destroyed,
> his dominion will never end.
> He rescues and he saves;
> he performs signs and wonders
> in the heavens and on the earth.
> He has rescued Daniel
> from the power of the lions.'
>
> *Daniel 6:26–27*

Certainly many great companies and institutions were founded by Christians and have been run on Christian principles – Rowntree's, Cadbury's, Lloyd's, Barclay's and Huntley & Palmer's to name but five established by Quaker families. There is no particular reason why the same cannot happen today.

Maybe not everyone in your workplace will become a Christian but perhaps you can work and pray to see it run on lines that reflect justice and mercy and respect for other people so that your co-workers will, like Darius, give praise to the living God.

Clocking on with God

The issue for us is that our God and our identities do not change when we walk through the factory gates. Indeed, it may well be that to be fruitful ministers in our workplace we don't actually need any startling new ideas. Rather we simply need to apply what we already know from other areas of our life to our workplace.

Samson discovers that the spirit of God is just as powerful on Philistine territory as he is within the borders of Israel. Indeed, he discovers that the spirit of God has just as much freedom to work in the very temple of the Philistine idol Dagon as he did in Judah. But do we feel that God is as powerful in the factory as at the church? As much Emmanuel, God with us, at work as at home?

Jacob, fleeing from the revenge of his brother, beds down on the road to Haran with a stone for a pillow. God appears to him in a dream and confirms the promises he had made to his father and grandfather. Waking, Jacob says:

> 'Surely, the Lord is in this place and I was not aware of it.'
>
> *Genesis 28:16*

Perhaps like Jacob we need to wake up and realise that God has not abandoned us at the factory gate like some parent dropping off his child at school. He is there. He is with us. And our resources are in no way diminished.

Surely, God is in your workplace.

Are you aware of it?

Surely, God's promises still apply.

Surely, God is with you there.

As he is with you everywhere.

4

The camomile factor
Or building relationships in love

'We must not, in thinking about how we can make a big difference, ignore the small daily differences we can make which, over time, add up to big differences we often cannot foresee.'

Marian Wright Edelman

Before you read this chapter you may want to consider writing down the names of three people with whom you believe God may want you to develop a deeper relationship.

Wimps and weirdos?

Christians don't have a very good image. On TV clergy are often portrayed as well-meaning, bumbling, absent-minded, slightly overweight, giggly wimps with secret weaknesses for sherry or cream cakes. The reality of the non-Christian's view is probably bleaker. Who, for example is describing whom in these research results?

These people are . . .
less free
more unfashionable
more isolated
less sexually fulfilled
more boring
psychologically weaker
with fewer interests
less realistic
less involved in the real world
less happy
less friendly . . .

That's the opinion of Newcastle students about Christians. (Taken from S M Boice, *Negative Attitudes to Christianity*.)

Building trust is vital in any relationship. And one barrier to developing trust is the preconceptions that many non-Christians have about Christians. So it is important to understand and face the non-Christian's attitude to Christians.

Here's how I think the average non-Christian working in London perceives the average Christian:

'Boring. They don't drink. They don't dance. They don't swear. They pretend not to have sex. They don't know how to have fun so they're trying to ruin it for the rest of us. They give away their money and go to church on Sundays as if it were a social club. Frankly, my golf club is more fun. And it's cheaper. The whole thing is a crutch. They are stupid and simple-minded. How can anyone really believe that stuff? It's superstitious mumbo jumbo. What's worse is that they're constantly trying to stuff it down our throats. Why should I accept it – I don't see any difference in their lives – Catholics, Protestants, born-again whatever. They're either fanatics or saccharine sweet. No spine. I've met one or two neat Christians, it's true, but most of them are weird. If that's what happens to Christians it's not a club I want to join. What would my friends think?'

That is pretty much what I thought about Christians before I became one. A huddle of mushy, simple-minded, ineffectual, well-meaning, boring, hypocritical, weird people. Sometimes the attitude still persists in me – and in others. For example, a while ago someone said to me of another Christian:

'I like spending time with her – I want to build up my base of Christians who are normal.'

If we are going to witness effectively we need to be aware of the preconceptions that the non-Christian holds. We need to recognise that there is some truth in those preconceptions and prepare ourselves to deal with them. At the same time we need to prepare ourselves to be thought weird, hypocritical and simpleminded. And not to care.

Silent light?

Still, if some non-Christians are suspicious, some are utterly indifferent. And others quite open. In any event we need to understand where they are coming from. And to determine that, whatever their views, we will neither become paranoid nor allow ourselves to be intimidated into silence. Of course, silence may for a while, even a long while, be the way the Spirit leads you. The path of silent witness should, however, not be the product of fear but rather the fruit of closeness to God.

Our understanding of our co-workers' suspicion, their fear of being trapped by a Christian fanatic should make us careful about how we talk about church and church-related activities. It may make us careful about bringing up religion before we have established a basis for friendship, but we should never let it stop us talking about Christ in a natural way. Most people can tolerate a little talk about Jesus. We simply need to know how and when to change the subject. Particularly perhaps in the early stages of a relationship, a swift change of topic can build tremendous trust. A non-Christian probably expects you to have the tenacity of a bulldog once the subject of religion comes up. Not pushing it early on may well give her the confidence to raise it herself or not to be put off if you mention it some other time.

Contaminating colleagues?

It is important not just that we recognise what our non-Christian co-workers think of Christians, but that we recognise what we, in turn, really think of them. What is our view of their lifestyle?

Superficial, self-destructive, empty, unfulfilling, contaminating? Something to flee from? Something to be afraid of? The consequence of such thinking is that many mature Christians retreat into a Christian ghetto, into splendid isolation. Most of their friends are Christians. Almost all of their disposable time is spent with Christians.

This attitude impairs evangelism in two ways:
1 Christians don't spend time with non-Christians outside the workplace so non-Christians are not exposed as much to the love of the gospel.
2 Non-Christians in the workplace sense the distance, sense the judgement that is being passed on them by Christians. This builds a barrier.

When I worked in the United States I always had much more success in relating to American women than to American men. I think the primary and not very original reason for this is that I prefer women. But why did I not have much success with American men? Well, superficially, it was because the stereotypical American man drinks a lot of beer, talks about baseball, his last round of golf, is dismissive of women, denies his feelings and knows nothing about the really important things in life – like cricket. The macho man. I have never felt particularly drawn to this sort of person. Do I have to go drink a lot of beer, learn baseball trivia and stop talking about cricket? No. But someone helped me to realise that the real reason I could not witness effectively to American men was that I was passing judgement on them. And the reason for that was that *I* felt inadequate. After all, American women marry these characters by the million. So this beer-swilling, baseball-talking machismo must be what they want. I would not accept American men for what they are because I didn't accept myself. Because I felt inadequate to compete with them for the fair or dark hands of millions of American women. Irrational. Stupid. But true. My problem.

How often do Christians avoid going to discos, not because they are dens of iniquity (though some of them are) or because they have developed a conviction about not dancing, but because they don't know how to dance and therefore feel uncomfortable?

How often do we avoid inviting someone over for supper, not because we don't like her, but because we think she will find our Christian friends boring and that we will have nothing to talk about?

Down with the barriers

The barrier to building relationships with non-Christians is often *not* their debauchery, but our fear, our neuroses, our inadequacies, our fear of rejection, of embarrassment, of being thought weird, of having nothing to talk about. We have to get right with ourselves, we have to recognise that we are worthy. And that will give us the confidence to meet non-Christians on their ground, as Christ did. We have to realise God loves them just the way they are. *And* that he loves us just the way we are.

Often the non-Christian will test us, will tell incredibly filthy jokes or swear more than usual, just to see how we will react. Will we crumble under the onslaught? Will we condemn him? Perhaps there is sometimes a need to challenge but often the most effective method is simply not to behave in the same way yourself. Ted Cobden was a Christian who worked with me. When he came he was very junior and very mature in God. Almost from his first day, before anybody knew he was a Christian, nobody swore round him – despite his lowly rank. Why? Ted never rebuked anybody. Mainly I think people just sensed something about him, something gentle and tender. And perhaps, subconsciously at first, they noticed he didn't swear. The power of example.

Christ at work

In developing relationships, Christ's example is instructive. His behaviour was often startlingly at odds with the culture that surrounded him. For example, three things non-Christians believe about Christians are:

1 They go to church.
2 They don't drink.
3 They choose their friends wisely.

But what did Christ do?

1 He was accused of breaking the Sabbath.
2 He drank wine.
3 He went to parties with publicans and sinners (Mark 2:15–17).

Indeed at the gathering in Mark's Gospel, there is no record of Jesus sharing the Good News. He spent time with people – on their territory. And what is interesting is that they invited him. They seemed to like having him around. He obviously did not inhibit them or judge them or sit in a corner to avoid contamination. Jesus was able to break the conventions of the religious leaders around him, without sinning. Similarly, some of us will need to question whether the church conventions which make us feel that there are certain places we can't go are actually ones that we should continue to follow. The pub is after all one of the main places people meet in our culture. Going for a drink, albeit a Perrier, at lunchtime may be precisely the right way to develop a relationship with a co-worker. That said, there is an important issue of conscience here and those who don't feel able to, shouldn't. And shouldn't be made to feel guilty.

Beyond understanding our co-workers, there is the call to serve them.

Let's look at the way Jesus serves non-believers:

In John 5 he takes the initiative and approaches and heals a paralytic but does not identify himself. He helps out with a physical problem.

In John 6, he feeds five thousand people. He takes on a responsibility that is clearly not his, anymore than it would be your responsibility to feed five thousand people who happened to crash your picnic in Hyde Park.

Yes, Jesus preaches and teaches but, quite independent of preaching and teaching, he takes initiatives and meets people's needs.

Ministry meets needs
What are the needs of the people around you at work?

Do you know? What are the felt needs of the three people you have written down? Well, here are some of the things that Christians ministered to at my old company, some of the problems that their co-workers were facing:
– divorce
– cancer in the family
– a husband's heart attack
– the end of a love affair
– a decision about marriage
– a thirty five year old psychological problem

- an invisible but incurable sexually transmitted
  disease
- separation
- bringing up a child as an unmarried mother

Today, the list would almost certainly also include things like:

- money
- debt
- fear of unemployment.

We relate to people at work primarily through our work but we must not forget that they are people and we must not flee from their pain.

Ministry is love in action. Ministry is bringing the whole gospel – in all its power and light and love – into the workplace. When a minister sees a need – he seeks to meet it. The parable of the Good Samaritan is, after all, not only a response to the question 'Who is my neighbour?' but also an answer to the unposed question 'Who is a minister?' And you are the minister. Ministry is love in action and, love, according to 1 Corinthians 14:1 is our aim. All the skills in the world will make little impact unless we have genuine concern for our neighbours who don't know Jesus.

And our neighbour is the lady at the next wordprocessor, the man in the next office, the person behind the cafeteria check-out, our boss.

Taking the initiative – with love

Observing particular needs is not enough. Some observations can be turned into prayer. In other cases we need to take initiatives to build trust. Initiative is very important. We cannot sit back and expect people to come to us. Jesus consistently took the initiative. He went to people, he asked questions, he came to die for us. We did not invite him. Love takes the initiative.

And lovers are extremely creative and resourceful. Love goes to every shop in town to find the chocolates that she adores. Love finds the right card, love makes time.

The camomile factor

Here are two examples of people taking the initiative to communicate love, to build relationships.

Craig Miller, a banker, decided that he would get a colleague in his department a birthday cake, stick a candle on it and go and make a fuss of him. Unprecedented in that particular bank. It just wasn't done. But who could object to a birthday cake? The Christian breaking down cultural barriers, gently pushing at the conventions which depersonalise the working environment. The Christian saying – it need not be this way.

Emily, a small Chinese lady, works at the United Nations. One day one of her co-workers, a fairly large lady, was not feeling well. 'Can I get you a cup of tea?' Emily enquired. 'No,' the other lady replied rather shortly, 'I don't like the tea here. I only drink camomile.' Emily left her, quietly slipped on her coat, took the lift down several floors and went down the street to a nearby shop. She returned with a box of camomile tea and gave it in her small hand to this large lady who immediately enveloped her in a huge hug, exclaiming, 'Emily, I love you.' Emily replied, rather muffled from the epicentre of this massive hug, 'I love you too.'

Emily's story illustrates a number of important points:

1 Be ministry minded – listen.

Emily could have just smiled and gone on her way. Instead, because she is ministry-minded, because she listened, because she saw the other person's need and desire, she took an initiative which totally transformed that person's mood and day.

2 Time is on *your* side, the opportunities will come.

We don't have to create situations in which we can minister. They will happen all by themselves. We are going to be in the workplace for a long time, we don't need to be anxious about finding opportunities. We simply have to pray and be alert.

3 Ministry is to individual people.

Obviously, camomile tea would not have been a good idea for everyone. We have talked about general principles and stereotypical non-Christian attitudes to the Christian, but each of us deals with individuals, so we must seek to study the habits, needs and desire of those individuals. It's going to be different in each case.

How much do you know about the three people you've written down? What is their favourite food? Their favourite hobby? How do they like their coffee? What is their most serious concern?

4 Ministry does not demand as it gives.

Emily asked for nothing, not even the money for the tea. Like the good Samaritan, she simply gave, expecting nothing in return. Our expressions of love for others should not have evangelistic strings attached. Emily did not give the lady a Bible with the tea or use it as an excuse to invite her to a Bible study. We must be tactful and sensitive as we love, and distinguish between the opportunities to serve and the opportunities to communicate the gospel verbally.

But do think about these little things.

A thank you note. An apology for a sharp word. Asking forgiveness is not only a biblical imperative, it is also so rare that it is an extremely powerful witness – though naturally, we should not do it just for that reason. A note of encouragement in someone's top drawer. A card for Easter. For the Chinese New Year. A newspaper clipping on a favourite topic. The offer, if someone is working late, to help out or to go get a sandwich. Food is almost always helpful. And, at the appropriate time, you can become just a little bolder.

For example, a lady called Jill, who worked for me and who had only just become a Christian, used to buy our boss his morning bran muffin on her way into work. One day she left a verse with it, presumably on the theory that man cannot live by bran muffin alone. She just didn't know that you are not meant to witness to your boss's boss, so she did. A small act, but at the time, a very brave one. A risk, he might have been offended. She judged right and God was gracious. He was not offended. And then she invited him to read the Bible with her. She just did not know that baby Christians are not meant to do that. It was not long before our boss became a believer. A little step. Take one.

These are the little everyday things that transform the work environment, that turn it into a place people enjoy. We should be diligent in expressing love. Is there some little thing you could do for someone next week?

Love in actions
The interesting thing about these little things is that they catch on – people start to follow suit. Don't worry that this is not directly communicating the plan of salvation, remember you are an expression of the gospel and when you put a mint on someone's desk, you communicate I John 3:18:

> 'Dear children, let us not love with words or tongue but with actions and in truth.'

When you don't grumble and complain, you communicate Philippians 2:14–16:

> 'Do everything without complaining or arguing, so that you may become blameless and pure, children of God without fault in a crooked and depraved generation, in which you shine like stars in the universe as you hold out the word of life . . .'

And you communicate these verses in a form that cannot be tuned out. The non-Christian can ignore almost every direct communication of the gospel, but he cannot ignore you wandering around filled with the fruits of the Spirit (Galations 5: 22–24).

Sometimes you can give someone a book that has a Christian perspective on an issue that he is dealing with – bereavement, raising kids, depression in the family, who to marry, whether to stay married. It may not be C S Lewis' *Mere Christianity* but it may clearly show him how relevant and helpful the Bible is to the everyday problems of life. One evening I was leaving the office and met someone who used to work with me in the lift. We chatted. She told me she was trying to work out whether to marry this man who had proposed to her.

By coincidence perhaps, I happened to have a copy of Jack and Carole Mayhall's *Marriage Takes More than Love* with me. I gave it to her. I saw her again on Monday. She'd read the whole thing, had accepted its perspective on marriage, though not on the gospel, and it had helped her to see why this particular man was not right for her. She wanted a copy for him.

By coincidence perhaps, I happened to have another one with me. They didn't get married. And as far as I know she hasn't yet become a Christian but I hope that the seed planted will bear fruit. I couldn't have given her a Bible at that point but I could give her something relevant to her life situation.

So take initiatives in love.

Using the way you work

Obviously not everyone could have left her office as Emily did and gone and bought camomile tea. The culture changes from office to office but in each situation there are probably some times and opportunities that are particularly conducive to developing relationships.

In my own case the way we worked was very helpful for developing good relationships. I spent a lot of time in meetings with people, a lot of time travelling with people and a lot of time with my immediate boss and those working with me. So I got to know them quite well. And I had my own office so it was easy to talk more personally if that's the way the conversation turned. At some stages in my career, lunchtime provided a regular opportunity to spend time with people. At others I had to work through lunch or my schedule was too unpredictable to make arrangements. Our circumstances change. But are we looking for opportunities?

Mark is a lawyer who spends most of his time working on his own. There are not many meetings and he does not travel. How does he develop relationships? He is going to have to take deliberate steps to make time to get to know his co-workers.

Craig is a banker and works in an open-plan office which makes it hard to let conversations flow into personal areas, but he does travel and lunch is a good time for him to develop relationships with those around him.

When are the times in your workplace when it is appropriate to develop relationships? Is it after work over a drink? Do you need to join one of the company sports teams? Or determine to have lunch with one of your three people once a month?

Do pray about what initiatives you could take to build trusting relationships.

5

Edge without guilt
Or getting the message out

'She was reading her Bible in the canteen. Which is a pretty brave thing to do. People think you're a nuthead if you're a Christian.'
Katriina Greene, Nurse

● S N A P S H O T ●

Clumsy for Christ

Five of us were on a two day trip out of town. Surely with all that time God would give me an opportunity to share something with someone. No opportunity came, or at least none that I could see. The time came to fly home. The client and I decided to work together on the plane. So, briefcase in hand, I negotiated my way into the window seat. As I lifted my case over the seat rest the lid came open and out tumbled about twenty small orange booklets ... 'Oh, no,' I thought. Twenty copies of a tract called *The Four Spiritual Laws* scattered over the floor and on the seats in front of me and my client. I felt like a teenager caught with some improper publication. I began to pick them up.

Then the very worst thing that could have happened actually happened.

The client said, 'What are those?'

'Errrrrrrrrrrrrrrrrrrrrrrrrrrrr ... they're little booklets which explain the main points about Christianity.'

I waited for a look of embarrassment. Or perhaps pity. Or discomfort.

'Oh, that's interesting,' she said, with a genuinely interested and open expression on her face, 'I've been thinking a lot about that recently. Could I have a look?'

The great dread

Witnessing is a guilt-edged word that fills many Christians with dread, particularly in the context of secular employment. Some of this dread has to do with natural nervousness, with fear of rejection or lack of confidence.

Some of this dread may also have to do with an incomplete understanding of witnessing as simply the verbal delivery of the gospel message, telling someone what the gospel is and challenging him to accept it. It is that. Or at least that is a critical component of witnessing and something we often try to avoid. But witnessing is more than just that. It is living the gospel in such a way that the difference it makes is communicated non-verbally. We witness verbally to the truth of the life, death, resurrection and ascension of Jesus but we witness in deed and character to the transformation that has occurred in our lives through what he has done for us. Jesus makes a difference. Unlike Muhammad, Jesus did not simply come to *bring* a message – he *was* the message. The word made flesh. And witnessing to him is living that message in our human flesh. It is being and doing and speaking.

Seeing is believing

The impact of the gospel is in significant measure communicated non-verbally as well as verbally. In his second letter to the Christians in Corinth, Paul says:

> 'You yourselves are our letter (of recommendation), written on our hearts, known and read by everybody. You show that you are a letter from Christ, the result of our ministry, written not with ink but with the Spirit of the

living God, not on tablets of stone but on tablets of human hearts.'

2 Corinthians 3:2–3

We are letters of recommendation. When people read us what do they see? We are Christ's advertisements in our workplace. Are we ads that speak to people of the divine, that suggest that there may be a better way? Or boring ads? That lack wit or boldness? As Marshall McLuhan said, the medium is the message and we are the medium. What is our message?

It is not only what we say but what we are. Robert Murray McCheyne wrote this to pastors but the principle applies to us all:

> 'Covet universal holiness of life. Your whole usefulness depends on this, for your sermons last but an hour or two; your life preaches all the week.'

Our lives are under constant scrutiny at work. We spend more time there than anywhere else. We spend more time with co-workers than anyone else. They see when we succeed, when we fail, when we remain joyful in tough circumstances, when we cancel social engagements, when we are asked to work on Sundays, when we are promoted, when we are tired and hungry. Our lives preach all the week.

Holiness at work

The world we live in puts an emphasis on techniques rather than on character. On results, on instant gratification, on tangible manifestations of success and on methods to achieve that success, on 'how to'. How to be happy. How to bring up children. How to have a happy wife. How to have a happy husband. Technique is important but not nearly as important as holy character. And holiness is not primarily an ethereal, otherworldy quality of misty peacefulness and beatific grins but rather the obedience that springs from love of God and love of one's neighbour. Several times in Leviticus 18–20, God says: 'Be holy because I, the Lord your God, am holy.' And then goes on to give a string of commandments which relate to idolatry, the occult, telling the truth, justice, business practice, feeding the poor, protecting resident foreigners and so on. Holiness works itself out in obedience to God across the whole range of human behaviour. Character works itself out in action. Both who we are and what we do are vital components of witnessing.

When someone is under pressure and has to work through lunch and we go and get him a sandwich, we bring this verse to life:

> 'Dear children, let us not love with words or tongue, but with actions and in truth.'
>
> *1 John 3:18*

When you don't fiddle your expenses even though lots of people do, you are illustrating Leviticus 19:11:

> 'Do not steal. Do not lie. Do not deceive one another.'

And don't believe it is not having an impact.

Legal expenses

Lewis Trippett was a lawyer working for a telephone company. One day a woman came in from the accounts department. He had never seen her before. She asked him if he was Lewis Trippett. With some trepidation, he replied, 'Yes, I am.' Then she said, 'You're the only one in this department with any integrity – don't change. Everyone else abuses their expenses.' Then as abruptly as he came she left. Little things make a difference.

In Matthew 5:16, Jesus says:

> 'In the same way, let your light shine before men, that they may see your good deeds and praise your Father in heaven.'

Now, it does not say:

> 'Let your *good works* so shine before men that they may see your light and give glory to your Father in heaven.'

The emphasis is not on the works but on the light. This is a vital distinction. What we want people to see is the light and the true God behind it, not our works. Similarly, John in his Gospel talks about Jesus' miracles as signs, pointers to his identity. The miraculous works point to the light.

Both Cain and Abel bring sacrifices to God. One brings sheep and one brings groceries. One is pleasing to God and one is not. That has nothing to do with the produce but rather with the character of the man. It is not just what we do but how we do it that determines the extent to which it brings glory to God.

Being 'Frank'

In the building where I used to work there was a lift operator called Frank. He stood at the bank of lifts in the main entrance and ensured that there was an even balance of lifts going up and lifts coming down. For many people this might be a menial, repetitive task with little opportunity to shine. But day in, day out, Frank would have a smile for everyone as they came in to work. Frank would greet us by name. He seemed to know all our names. And he would tell us to have love in our hearts.

Frank was a lift operator but people did not see menial drudgery in his job. They saw in it an opportunity to transmit love and joy, to make people look forward to their day, and help them overcome the frustrations of their journey into work. One person even walked round the block to come in at Frank's entrance so she could start her day with a warm welcome from Frank. I don't know whether Frank was a Christian but people saw his job in the light of his cheerful, giving spirit. When he retired my company gave him a significant chunk of our shares. And he didn't even work for us – he worked for the owner of our office building. He made a difference.

So it is with our work. What light do we want it to be seen in? Ideally, we want people to see in our work the light that Jesus has brought into our lives. What we do and the way we relate to people should point others to God. Excellence, which we will discuss later, does not in itself do that. Excellence is not necessarily the exclusive province of God's children, nor is good character, nor is honesty. Somehow, by grace, by the power of the Spirit to transform us, to work in us, there must be something about our light that points to God.

Pharaoh's praise

Joseph is a good example. His discernment so shone before Pharaoh that Pharaoh gave him the name Zaphrah-paneah which means 'God is living'. Indeed, it is precisely because Pharoah recognised God's revelation in Joseph's wisdom that he put Joseph in charge of Egypt. Pharaoh said to his servants:

'Can we find anyone like this man, one in whom is the spirit of God?'

Then Pharoah said to Joseph, 'Since God has made all this known to you, there is no one so discerning and wise as you. You shall be in charge of my palace, and all my people are to submit to your orders.'

Genesis 41:38–39

God's revelation of the meaning of Pharaoh's dreams was a one-off supernatural event but it was followed by a lifetime of faithfulness and wisdom. Certainly God does intervene in supernatural ways as he did in Joseph's life, and we may or may not give him the glory. However, he also has the opportunity to reveal himself through our character, through our response to everyday events. Our lights can shine, our testimony to the power of the gospel can be powerful, without the direct verbal communication of the Good News.

How God is going to use you in the process of bringing those around you to himself is up to him and you. In one case you may do something that may not truly register for another decade, in another you may lead someone to the Lord. In another you may encounter some hostility. One person hoes, one person sows, one person waters. But he will use you, whether or not you are always aware of it.

Think for a moment of the way God brought you to himself. Certainly there may be one or two people who were particularly significant. And there may be people who you have completely forgotten who taught you something important. But maybe in heaven you will know the impact they had.

Equally there are probably people who did things that struck you or people who said something that made a big impact on you. And they will never know, at least not till heaven, the difference they made.

Victory tea

When I was a student and not yet a Christian my college hockey team had an end of season tea. A couple of the team were Christians and they volunteered to host the occasion. They laid on a sumptuous feast. They also laid on something I, at least, did not expect. Maybe I had missed an announcement or a note somewhere along the line. Anyway there we all were, twelve or thirteen hockey players, good and true, and up pops a missionary.

I was probably a little irritated. I suppose he must have given us a talk. I don't remember. What I do remember is that as the afternoon wore on we had a discussion about what happens to people who don't accept Christ as their saviour. I used to love debates and as the discussion progressed, I sniffed blood with all the glee of a piranha in a Bond movie. 'So,' I said, trying to conceal the thrill of anticipated triumph, 'what you're saying is that good rabbis go to hell.'

In the context of that gathering of people, this was a no-win situation for him.

If he said, 'Yes they do,' he would lose all credibility with the non-Christians, or so I thought.

If he said 'No,' then there was no need for a Jew like me to become a Christian.

If he pfaffed around and tried to duck the issue, he would be a pfaffer who had tried to duck the issue.

I can still remember the scene. He was sitting back in an armchair opposite me. He rubbed his left temple with his left hand and looked down at the floor. I waited on the edge of my seat. And then in reply to the question do all good rabbis go to hell, he said softly, almost sadly, 'Yes, I would have to say they do.'

I leant back, sated with my victory.

In heaven, no doubt, a thousand angels rejoiced in his.

To me, it looked like he had lost. To others around me, I suspect it looked like that too. Today I would agree with him. Today I admire him for his courage and his conviction. For being more concerned about the truth than winning a debating point or two. I still remember that incident vividly. I don't know his name. I've never seen him since. God used him. Sometimes it looks like we lose. It looks like we lose in public. It looks like we are fools. Sometimes looks deceive.

One sows, another waters, another reaps.

Evangelism is not just about decisions. It is not just about giving someone the opportunity to make a decision for Christ. It is about being involved in the process of bringing someone along on the road from negativity or indifference to a positive decision for Christ. So we need to have confidence in God, that he is in fact working in us and through us in the process of bringing others to him.

A wasted holiday?

Katriina was a nurse and had studied and worked with Renata for two years. Katriina was a Christian, Renata wasn't. The local Christian fellowship had planned a one week ski trip and Katriina felt strongly that she was meant to ask Renata along. One week before the trip, Katriina pulled some ligaments in her left leg and it was put in a cast. Not exactly the ideal physical condition for downhill skiing. Katriina decided not to go. Renata didn't want to go without her.

Katriina prayed about the issue. She decided to go

on the trip, to take the time and invest the money, even though she herself would spend most of the week with her leg resting on a stool inside a chalet, listening to stories of how good the snow was and how exhilarating that turn by the trees was and how wonderfully tired everybody felt. But she was convinced that it was important for Renata to go.

That week Renata became a Christian.

Katriina didn't lead her to Christ herself but it was Katriina who obeyed God and who sacrificed time and money to ensure that Renata heard the gospel that week. God used her in the process.

Gospel perspectives on general issues

Evangelism is a process. And the reality that the Bible is relevant to every area of life can be demonstrated in conversations on almost any topic even if no biblical text is mentioned.

If you're a TV watcher you can chat to people about the storylines in your favourite soap operas and the particular issues they are exploring at the time – AIDS, homosexuality, adultery. What should Bobbi do when she discovers that Greg is having an affair? Are homosexual relationships OK, as EastEnders argued so persuasively?

Sometimes the news provides a clear opportunity for discussion. In 1993 Britain was rocked by the brutal murder of a two year old boy, James Bulger, by two ten year olds. The details that emerged from the trial day by day transfixed the nation. It seemed to many that our society had reached a new depth of darkness. How could such a thing happen in 90s Britain? Press commentators seemed bewildered or forced into concluding, as one newspaper headline did, that James's murderers were 'freaks of nature'. Here, in this tragic event, was an opportunity to speak about what the Bible has to say about the nature of human beings. Here in this tragic event was an opportunity to ask what future there might be for the two ten year old murderers if they do not experience forgiveness. Here, in this tragedy for James's parents and family was an opportunity to ask what future there is for them if they cannot forgive the ghastly crime committed against their little son. In short as Britain reeled at the daily bad news from the courtroom there were probably millions of opportunities in canteens and bus queues, over coffee or lunch, to talk about the nature of humanity and the Good News of Jesus.

Gospel perspectives on personal issues

The Bible has something to say on virtually every issue in life that people face. And the people you work with are facing issues. Research suggests, for example, that many people in London are beset by a sense of purpose-lessness in their lives. On the surface life may be fine but underneath, as one UK Billy Graham advertising campaign put it, 'Who can make sense of it?'

And beyond a sense of purposelessness there may be anxiety about redundancy, bereavement perhaps, a recent divorce, whether to continue that affair, illness in the family. It's not our business to pry. It's not part of our job description to become the company agony aunt but it may be part of our role as Christians to be the kind of person that people can talk to about problems. And the two most important things we need are an open ear and a tender heart. 'All the lonely people, where do they all come from?' sang the Beatles in 1966. The situation hasn't improved over the years. Indeed, loneliness is a chronic disease in our society. Many people are yearning just for someone to listen to them.

And if we listen carefully then perhaps we will find the right word to say at the right time. Perhaps we'll be able to bring a biblical perspective to bear on the issue.

Sometimes we'll find ourselves totally out of our depth, inadequate for the task. In this I am much encouraged by the story Jesus tells in Luke's Gospel chapter 11. It's worth quoting in full:

> 'Suppose one of you has a friend, and he goes to him at midnight and says, "Friend, lend me three loaves of bread because a friend of mine on a journey has come to me, and I have nothing to set before him." Then the one inside answers, "Don't bother me. The door is already locked, and my children are with me in bed. I can't get up and give you anything." I tell you, though he will not get up and give him the bread because he is his friend, yet because of the man's boldness he will get up and give him as much as he needs.
> 'So I say to you: Ask and it will be given to you; seek and you will find; knock and the door will be opened to you. For everyone who asks receives; he who seeks finds; and to him who knocks, the door will be opened.'
>
> *Luke 11:5–10*

The story is not just about persistence in prayer. It also makes the point that if I bring my friend to God in prayer God will answer. I don't have the resources but God does. And he will respond. What an encouragement!

Gospel perspectives on business issues

The Bible has something to say about how we do the work we do. And as Christians we need to work out not just what it means to be a Christian in accountancy but what it means to be a Christian accountant. That is, how does my personal faith affect my public work? A Christian advertising executive, for example, will not only have to ask himself whether his ads are honest, decent, legal and truthful according to current social standards but whether his ads are honest, decent, legal and truthful according to God's standards.

What perspectives on your work does the Bible bring to bear? On how to motivate people? On bringing up children? On how to sell? On being a mechanic? On Total Quality Management? If we want to change companies and industries for the better we will have to wrestle with the issues that they face and look for answers from the Bible. Making such an effort is really quite rare and there is a deep need for people in similar jobs to get together to work through these issues. And a deep need for our ministers to help us. And a crying need for our theological colleges to train them to do so.

Getting the message out

Successful sports teams and successful businesses tend to have one thing in common – they know what they're there to do, which is to win games or to make products people will pay for. They know their objectives. But in our ministries it is easy to forget our overall objectives. For example:

- To bring glory to God through our work.
- To help people to know Christ.
- To make disciples.

These may seem very obvious on paper but they are not so obvious in practice. Day by day. Apparently the most common mistake professional salespeople make is that they don't ask for the sale. And perhaps one of the most common mistakes that Christians make is that they never ask their friends or co-workers if they would like to become followers of Jesus.

I had been in my job at Ogilvy and Mather for four years. In my first two and a half years, I probably shared my personal testimony over thirty times. I was involved in an early morning meeting with a non-Christian, and another one with two Christians. I developed a number of solid friendships which I still have today. I prayed and I gave away a lot of books.

Sounds pretty good, doesn't it?

In that time, however, no one at Ogilvy and Mather became a Christian.

After two and a half years, the total number of known Christians at Ogilvy was five. About 0.3% of the corporate population. An evangelistic need greater than the one million Bambara in the Ivory Coast, the 350,000 Dagomba in Ghana, the two million Acehnese in North Sumatra. In fact, an evangelistic need greater than almost every ethnic group on earth. Fortunately, only my company was paying for my missionary efforts.

In the nine months that followed, the ministry grew dramatically. Three separate quiet time groups started meeting in the mornings. A man called Ted began a Bible Study, a prayer chain with ten people was set up, three people were involved in a 14 week Bible Study after work in someone's flat. An excited recommitted Christian woman appeared and quietly started developing a ministry, and, in response to prayer for more workers, a mature Christian man emerged. And four people became Christians.

At the spiritual level God clearly intervened. Perhaps, too, we were reaping the fruit of three years' work and prayer. We did pray. We not only prayed, we prayed for growth. For more Christians to come. For more workers to come. And they came.

And we did actually ask people the crucial question – do you want this? We do communicate the gospel through our behaviour but at some point people need to hear the word. People need information to make a decision for Christ. In the nine fruitful months, I gave away ten copies of the longish gospel tract *The Four Spiritual Laws* (it's now been renamed *Do you want to know God personally?*) and I went through the material with three people. All three became Christians.

We must give people the information they need to make a decision. And we must ask them if they want to decide for Christ. This has nothing to do with high pressure guilt manipulation. It is simply taking the initiative to ask them what is after all a natural and vital question – do you want Jesus in your life?

So from time to time it's good to consciously remind ourselves of why we're at work and to ask ourselves what fruit we have seen.

- Has anyone come to Christ?
- Have we seen any change in attitudes?
- Have we been able to develop a relationship with anyone?
- Have we had an opportunity to share the gospel with anyone?
- Is there another Christian co-worker we could pray with?
- Have we been praying for opportunities for growth?

The problem for many of us is that we will do almost anything rather than directly share the gospel with someone and ask if he is interested. I used to get quite tense as I got to that point in a conversation and often had to force myself forward, even though there was nothing in the other person's behaviour to indicate that he didn't want me to go on. Certainly there may be some kind of spiritual warfare when we get close to sharing the gospel with someone – it is, after all, not in Satan's best interests to see Christ's kingdom growing in citizens. Sometimes we put our reticence down to Britishness. We're not pushy. Or we call it sensitivity, when sometimes it's just plain cowardice. But the irony is that very often people want us to tell them about Jesus.

Holy boldness

Still, we need to recognise that it does take courage to share the Good News. And this particular brand of courage is precisely the kind that the Holy Spirit is in the habit of providing. In the Book of Acts two characteristics keep recurring in the description of the early disciples – joy and boldness. Often when they speak out, Luke records that they do so with boldness. Here's the response of the Sanhedrin after hearing Peter's speech in Acts 4:

> When they saw the *boldness* of Peter and John and realised that they were unschooled, ordinary men, they were astonished and they took note that these men had been with Jesus.
>
> *Acts 4:13*

In 4:29 Peter prays these words:

> 'Now, Lord, consider their threats and enable your servants to speak your word with *great boldness*.'

In verse 31 it says that the prayer was answered,

> 'And they were all filled with the Holy Spirit and spoke the word of God *boldly*.'

Look too at Acts 9:27,29; 13:46; 14:3; 18:26; 19:8. This kind of boldness is not self-confidence. It is not the product of an extrovert personality type but of the Holy Spirit. God isn't asking us to change our personalities, he's asking us to make ourselves open to his Spirit. Boldness can be gentle. Boldness can come with a winsome smile. But it is unlikely to be silent. And only the Spirit can give it to us.

Ready, steady, tongue-tied?

One common barrier to telling people about the gospel is not feeling confident that you can explain it in simple, jargon-free language that is understandable to someone who hasn't ever set foot in a church. This is probably a common problem. First, it's worth saying that it is better to struggle to communicate the truth about Jesus than not to try to communicate it at all. Second, witnessing does not have to be in the form of a prepared lecture – it can be just like a conversation between two people.

On one occasion, I was having a meal in a coffee shop and as I left I said to the waitress, 'I don't know if you're interested but this is something about Jesus, that you might find interesting,' and I offered her a little booklet. (It wasn't a great speech. Notice the repetition of 'interest' in two different forms). But anyway she replied, 'Oh yes, I belong to him.' She witnessed simply, concisely, powerfully, communicating something rich about her relationship with Jesus. She belonged to him. She was his. And she was happy about it. The words spoke of Jesus' Lordship. The matter-of-fact way she said them spoke of her trust in him and her love for him.

That's witnessing at its simplest, but the Bible encourages us to be ready to give an account of what we believe so it is worth thinking through how we might communicate the gospel to a non-Christian co-worker. There are a number of little booklets that set out various simple ways of communicating the gospel and you can practice on someone in your housegroup. Another helpful tool is to be able to tell someone how you became a Christian – again using non-technical language to do so. Don't worry if you don't have a spectacular 'drugs-to-sainthood' testimony. What will interest the non-Christian is that it is *your* story and that Christ is real to you.

Witnessing in the workplace is done in word and deed, with respect for the truth and compassion for the listener.

It is hard.

It seems to go against our British reserve to talk about anything as personal as religion. There was a time when there were three things the British didn't talk about over dinner – sex, politics and religion. Now there are only two – religion and death. So it can feel awkward.

At its best witnessing is the natural overflowing of our relationship with Jesus. We don't have to be perfect to share Jesus. We don't have to be the best at our job to share Jesus, but we do, as one Christian organisation expresses it, have to 'take the initiative to share the gospel in the power of the Spirit and leave the results to God.'

As the kids' chorus goes, 'Be bold, be strong, for the Lord your God is with you.'

Ain't it the truth.

EPILOGUE

All that glitters
Or a cautionary tale about witnessing

It had been a great conversation. I had felt free to talk to her at some length about Christ. She seemed attentive, interested, open. I was quite excited about what might happen next. It was Friday and she was going away for the weekend.

Come Tuesday there it was. I could hardly believe my eyes. There on a piece of paper stuck to her bookshelf for all to see were these words: 'He's alive, he's alive, he's alive'.

I said nothing. I didn't want to come across as over-eager or perhaps put her in a situation she wasn't ready for. But inside I was rejoicing. Imagine that: 'He's alive, he's alive, he's alive', the good news of the resurrection writ large in an advertising executive's office! Halleluiah!

A couple of months later I discovered that one of her friends had sent her the piece of paper and it referred not to Jesus but to another reputed sighting of the long dead King of Rock 'n Roll, Elvis Presley.

Things ain't always what they seem to be. But even though the conversation I'd had with her had not led at that time to a heartfelt conviction about Christ's resurrection, it was, from another point of view, a successful piece of witnessing. I'd taken 'the initiative to share the

Good News in the power of the Spirit'. The results, as always, are up to God.

6

Getting going
Or the twenty minute start-up programme

'Procrastination, they say, is the thief of time. And it doesn't do much for evangelism either.'

Verse and more

Christina loved literature so I gave her a copy of a seventeenth century poem called 'Love' by one of the great English poets. It's one of my very favourite poems. It's about Jesus as creator, as forgiver, as love, as encourager.

Love bade me welcome: yet my soul drew back,
        Guiltie of dust and sinne.
But quick-ey'd Love, observing me grow slack
        From my first entrance in,
Drew nearer to me, sweetly questioning,
        If I lack'd any thing.

A guest, I answer'd, worthy to be here:
        Love said, You shall be he.
I, the unkinde, the ungratefull? Ah, my deare,
        I cannot look on thee.
Love took my hand and smiling did reply,
        Who made the eyes but I?

Truth, Lord, but I have marr'd them; let my shame
        Go where it doth deserve.
And know you not, sayes Love, who bore the blame?
        My deare, then I will serve.
You must sit down, sayes Love, and taste my meat:
        So I did sit and eat.

George Herbert

She read it and loved it.

Just before she went on holiday I offered her a selection of four(!) books for her summer reading – from the heavily spiritual to the entertaining. She took one or two things. But I think I overdid it that time.

When we know people's interests we can find ways to expose them to the truth in ways that they may well enjoy. Whether it be a seventeenth century verse or something less highbrow and more contemporary like Steve Turner's poetry or rock music or . . .?

But do we know our co-workers that well?

DEVELOPING A MINISTRY PLAN

At the beginning of chapter 4 I suggested you write down the names of three people in your workplace that you think God might particularly want you to relate to on a spiritual level. Now is the time to apply the principles we've looked at about developing relationships to your three people. Why not pray now and work through the questions below for just one of them?

Some questions to consider about the person you are praying for

Don't worry too much if you don't know the answers to some of the questions – you don't need to know all these things to develop a relationship but some of the answers might indicate where you could start.

Stage 1
A. General questions

1 What kind of person is he? What are his chief characteristics?

2 What are his hobbies, main interests?

3 What do you have in common with him?

4 What do you like and dislike about him? What do you find difficult to accept about him?

B. Questions about values and attitudes to God

1 What do you think is most important to him?

2 How do you think he views God?

3 What do you think he thinks of Christianity?

4 What do you think he thinks of Christians?

5 What does he think of you?

6 What barriers do you feel there might be to him becoming a Christian?

7. What areas in his life (if any) do you think he feels are most in need of change?

8. What attitudes, beliefs, misconceptions does he need to change?

Stage 2
What specific things could you do to serve, help, encourage this person? In general? In spiritual development?

The questions may have indicated that you actually know very little about the person or they may have shown you that there are specific areas of life that the person is concerned about – a teenage son, being single, a sense of purposelessness, whatever. In turn that information may give you more ideas for:

- Prayer.

- Changing your attitude or behaviour towards him.

- Reading – so as to be able to address the issues that concern him from a Christian point of view.

- Asking other Christians for advice about particular issues.

- Giving/lending a book/article.

- Inviting him to a particular kind of event.

- Introducing him to a Christian friend with similar interests.

Stage 3
What do you want to happen next?

Stage 4
What steps are you going to take?

In the next week?

In the next month?

Within three months?

Obviously, it is important to pray about each of these steps and to continue to be open to the Holy Spirit as you move forward. There's no particular reason why the Lord should not give you a clear opportunity to share the gospel verbally with someone you really don't know that well. On the other hand, it may be that you know someone very well but that you feel the next step is simply to watch and pray. As Hamlet said, '. . . the readiness is all.'

Stage 5
Share your plan with someone else who is prepared to support you in prayer.

Stage 6

Come back to your answers in a month's time and evaluate:

What happened.

What you learned.

What you did.

What you have seen God doing.

The Lord give you wisdom and boldness as you seek to know and do his will.

7

The body business
Or the loneliness of the long-distance working Christian. And how to conquer it

'The lone wolf dines alone. And less often!'

'Though one may be overpowered, two can defend themselves. A cord of three strands is not easily broken.'

Ecclesiasties 4:12

'Each one should use whatever gift he has received to serve others, faithfully administering God's grace in its various forms.'

The Apostle Peter, 1 Peter 4:10

THE BODY BUSINESS

Christianity is a body business.

It's not about glorious individuals storming the strongholds of atheism and apathy and indifference like superspiritual Rambos. It's about the body of Christ working together. It's about supporting one another wherever God calls us as individuals. It's about putting our gifts at the service of one another so that the whole body grows. Praying for one another. Training one another. Working through some ethical issue together. Doing things for one another. Perhaps sometimes something highly practical and not obviously very spiritual – like someone's ironing because she has an opportunity to talk to a co-worker about Christ and needs some stuff ready for the morning. Or preparing the meal for the evangelistic Bible Study that someone else is going to lead in someone else's house.

1. Involving other Christians ... outside your workplace

> 'When it comes to my role as a Christian at work I feel unsupported by my fellowship.'
>
> *Wendy Somerville, Hospital Consultant*

Wendy isn't alone in that feeling.

Many Christians feel exactly the same way.

But Wendy is rare in actually expressing such a feeling. Many Christians don't expect there to be any interest in the spiritual dimensions of their work or their fellowship to support them in prayer. Except in times of crisis. The workplace and the people in it are not perceived as particularly significant, although much prayer will go into a leaflet campaign to invite people we don't know to a seeker service in the church. And appropriately so. This lack of corporate prayer for the workplace suggests that we may have accepted the division which our secular colleagues have drawn between the public world of nine to five, where our faith and our God are not meant to trespass, and the private world of five to nine where we can do what we like.

Wendy, I'm glad but somewhat ashamed to confess, is in my housegroup. She hadn't felt supported in her work by our group, though I think she would have felt supported in other areas of her life. Certainly, we had prayed for some specific situations – relationships and patient care and the restructuring of the Health Service – but actually we had only the sketchiest notion of what she did day by day, who she worked with, what kind of pressures she was under, what kind of issues she faced. So, one evening we asked her to give us a sketch of a day in her life. It took an hour. Some people's jobs are less complex and might have only taken ten minutes. But at the end of the time we had a much clearer picture of how Wendy spends sixty five percent of her life and therefore how we can pray for her.

But as a group we're not there yet.

Because we're still not asking the spiritual questions about work automatically. Nor seeking prayer from one another for work issues automatically. Nor challenging one another about ministry in our workplaces or wherever it is that God has put us. We need to reorient our thinking – not to make work issues the primary issues or even the dominant issues but rather to redress the balance so that people know that God and God's people are genuinely interested in the way they spend sixty five percent of their waking lives.

How can you involve other Christians in your ministry at work? And how can you encourage them in their ministry? Wherever it might be? If you're in a housegroup that might be the perfect context. You see one another regularly enough to share what's going on and to encourage one another in performance, relationships and ministry. Perhaps you might begin by having a regular ten minute slot focused on work for five or six weeks. After that, people may well have become sufficiently conscious of work issues for them to become a more natural part of what they share and what they ask others about. Or you might have a prayer partner you could share with. Or if you're married you might make a point of praying for one another's work, of making both workplaces matters for mutual concern. Even and perhaps especially, if one of them is actually the home.

2. Involving other Christians... in your workplace

There may well be other Christians in your workplace. If there are, you and they may find it very helpful to meet regularly to pray or talk through issues that you face in your work. Pray that God will lead you to them or bring other Christians into your workplace.

My first meetings were with a Roman Catholic guy and we read the Psalms together. Later I met mainly with non-Christians on a one to one basis. Then a number of Christians came to the firm and we began to meet weekly for prayer. That fizzled out a bit but then for a long time I met with another Roman Catholic man who had evangelism and encouragement very much on his heart. He kept me going. And he kept us praying.

Then I nervously asked the managing director to allow us to use a conference room for a monthly lunchtime meeting. He agreed and there were often a dozen or more at the meetings – with twenty five or thirty people on the 'mailing' list. After a couple of years that fizzled out.

Try things. Start things. Persevere. But feel free to stop things when they're not working for anyone.

Some people use the company noticeboard to advertise meetings. A friend of mine who's been in his current job just nine months did so and is now one of a group of five who meet weekly. It's encouraging for all the Christians there and it may well provide a safe first stop for someone who's mildly interested in Jesus but wouldn't set foot in a church for all the Guinness in Ireland.

Still, it takes courage to pin your name next to Jesus' on the company noticeboard. The moment you do you will probably feel somewhat vulnerable and start to think that everyone is looking at you strangely.

You may well be right.

8

Case Study: Romeo/ Juliet
Or love's labours won

'The path to hell may be paved with good intentions but the path to heaven is certainly strewn with mixed motives.'

CASE STUDY

Romeo/Juliet

Romeo/Juliet is whichever sex you are not.

27 years old. Pretty cute. University educated and smart. Says what he/she likes in a forthright but not unkind or aggressive manner. Nevertheless can be a bit intimidating. Comes from a Protestant background, but is not a churchgoer. Has a significant other who is pretty significant – been going out a couple of years. Not engaged. Has quite a few friends, some fairly longstanding. Likes movies, runs a literature group. Goes to the health club, likes to dance. Good at the job. Well-liked. Family lives in Surbiton.

1 How would you go about witnessing to this individual?

2 What particular challenges do you think you might face?

ROMEO/JULIET – WHAT HAPPENED

Juliet worked for me. Her name was Jill. I was single. I fell in love. There were at least three barriers to saying anything about it to her:

1 She worked for me.
2 She wasn't a Christian.
3 She had a boyfriend.

I prayed a lot for her. Every day for months, all kinds of prayers, all kinds of verses, telling myself and God that his will would be best. At one stage I persuaded myself by a convoluted piece of fanciful Scripture interpretation that God might be saying Jill was the one for me. I asked God to show me one way or another within six months. I'm not sure I'd give God those kind of deadlines now but I was young and in love. It was February 21st.

Then Jill stopped working for me.

One down.

Then she became a Christian.

Two down.

She hadn't left her boyfriend but on August 17th, in a gush of Elizabethan rhetoric, I told her how I felt about her.

On August 21st, six months to the day, Jill told me that she had split up with her boyfriend.

Three down.

She also told me, kindly but in no uncertain terms, that there was no way we were going to become an item.

God had answered my prayer.

I couldn't pretend to be grateful.

Four down.

Of course, I didn't believe her.

But she was right. I didn't turn out to be her Romeo. Nor she my Juliet.

The nuts and bolts of how she became a believer illustrate some important points about witness at work:
1 There was **exposure to a Christian**. However flawed I was, however selfishly motivated, I was there.

And it turned out that I was the right person for Jill – she had had a very negative view of Christians – stupid and no fun. Apparently I was neither. Every Monday, she used to ask me if I'd had a good weekend and I'd reply, 'Yes'. After a while this began to get to her. The issue here is not that I have an upbeat, happy-go-lucky, sometimes infuriatingly jolly, noisy and childish personality, the issue is that God put Jill in contact with the right person for *her*. But I didn't know at the time that she had a negative view of Christians – I was just there. So indeed it may well be that you, whatever your personality type and gifts, are just the right person for someone, or for quite a lot of the people, you work with right now. And you probably won't know that till afterwards.

2 There was **prayer**. However mixed my motives. I was at least trying to pray for her salvation and growth with no rings attached.

3 There was the development of a **relationship**, discussions about all sorts of things, eventually including spiritual matters. She heard the word. That involved me in some risk. I had to tell her at some point that I was a Christian. What would she think?

> 'So faith comes from what is heard, and what is heard comes by the preaching of Christ.'
>
> *Romans 10:7*

4 There was **exposure to the scriptures**. I invited her to read the Bible with me one morning a week before work for ten or fifteen minutes. She agreed. She read the word for herself.

5 One day I **shared the gospel** with her using a simple gospel plan. I challenged her. There was risk involved there too. In fact, I thought she accepted the Lord that day. Later, though, she told me it wasn't a genuine moment of commitment.

6 I invited her to a five week evangelistic Bible study with several other people. Further exposure to the word. More risk on my part – she was after all my subordinate and I certainly didn't want her to feel that

I was using my position to pressure her, a kind of evangelistic harassment. The study was subsequently extended for another six weeks or so and I involved Sandy, a mature Christian woman, of about Jill's age. There was the **witness of other Christians**. After the study ended, Sandy invited her and the other women in the group to a study. Jill agreed to go.

All this over about a fifteen month period.

God using exactly those tools that Jim Petersen points to in his book *Evangelism as a Lifestyle*:

1 The witness of the individual.
2 The witness of the word.
3 The witness of other Christians – the body.
4 The witness of the Spirit drawing Jill to himself.

And a fifth.

God's sovereign control over events.

At one point Jill had started to read Matthew's Gospel on her own and skip around churches a bit. But wherever she went there was a sermon on Matthew waiting just for her. This began to get to her – someone up there was trying to tell her something.

You may think you're alone in seeking to win someone to the Lord but there's a whole army of other Christians out there God might use. And all the ingenuity of his creative mind and his awesome Spirit. And even if you are alone, one plus God, as Elijah demonstrated so clearly in his confrontation with the prophets of Baal and Asherah, is a distinct majority.

> 'Not by might nor by power, but by my Spirit,' says the Lord.
>
> *Zechariah 4:6*

Finally, this case illustrates something very important.

Evangelism is not an event.

It is not just something that happens when the Good

News is shared and Christ invites someone into his kingdom.

Evangelism is not an event.

It is a process.

The Spirit moving a person from where they are through all kinds of means towards their own encounter with Jesus.

Jill became a Christian. So did our boss David. God used us both. But most of the people that we worked with, and prayed for and witnessed to, haven't become Christians. Or, at least, not yet.

But evangelism is a process – only God knows how *he* will use our witness, how *your* witness will contribute in the future. As Paul points out in his first letter to the Christians in Corinth:

> What, after all is Apollos? And what is Paul? Only servants, through whom you came to believe – as the Lord has assigned to each his task. I planted the seed, Apollos watered it, but God made it grow. So neither he who plants nor he who waters is anything, but only God, who makes things grow.
>
> *1 Corinthians 3:5–7*

Prayer, initiative, risk – and God at work.

9

Work is a seven letter word

Or a whiff of excellence is worth a ton of mediocrity

'They didn't want it good. They wanted it on Wednesday.'

Robert Heimleur

Pastor C H Spurgeon once asked a young girl, who served as a domestic in one of his families . . . what evidence she could give of having become a Christian, and she meekly answered, 'I now sweep under the mats.'

From *The Family Friend*, 1885
S W Partridge & Co

SNAPSHOT

The Accidental Birth of a Hero

When I was about eighteen I went to spend nine months working on a kibbutz. I was looking forward to the outdoor life, the sunshine on my face, the soil beneath my feet and the fruit trees all around.

My first job was doing the dishes.

Inside.

The electric light on my face. The tiles beneath my feet. And the walls all around.

About an hour or so into the job someone brought over a huge stainless steel ovenrack. It probably had twenty shelves on it. 'Give that a clean will you.' It was filthy. It looked to me as if it hadn't been cleaned properly in about a decade. Encrusted with goo, hardened by a million hours in the oven at high temperatures, its essential colour was not gleaming silver but browny black. Resentfully, I began to clean it. After a while I realised it was going to take me a couple of hours. My resentment began to build. I felt that these kibbutzniks were taking advantage of this new foreigner, giving me a job no one else had been bothered to do for weeks.

Maybe months.

Maybe years.

Maybe since the day it was bought.

After about an hour and a half I was getting really angry. But I carried on. There didn't seem much choice. 'Wow,' said the person who gave me the job, as she saw how the stainless steel had emerged from fifteen or so of the racks, 'I only meant give it a quick wipe.'

The word went round the kibbutz that I was an outstanding worker. Rather like the glorious Charge of the Light Brigade, it was just a terrible misunderstanding.

But I never told them that.

THE PURSUIT OF EXCELLENCE

Billy Graham's wife probably has a different attitude. I've never been to her house but the story goes that she has a plaque above her kitchen sink which reads: 'Divine services conducted here three times daily.'
Work is ordained by God. And it should be dedicated to God. As we saw earlier the Hebrew word for work is *avodah*, the same as the word for worship. 'Service' captures the flavour best. Work is a seven letter word – service – to God and people. And though I would lose my job if I built a theology on the basis of that observation alone we can see elsewhere in scripture that work is part of the 'everything' we do 'to the glory of God'. For God, work is part of our worship. It is part of our service to him.

We submit our work not just to our earthly boss but to our heavenly boss, God. Here's Paul writing to first century slaves:

> Whatever you do,
> **work at it**
> **with all your heart**,
> **working for**
> **the Lord**,
> not for
> men.
>
> *Colossians 3:23*

And God could hardly expect us to work 'with all our heart' unless the work itself was of some significance to *him*. Some tasks may not seem very important to the people in your organisation but they are important to God. Work is not just a platform for evangelism and ministry. It is significant in itself. And that's why its quality is important. How good is the work you do? Good enough to be offered to God? Pause a moment and think not of your job as a whole but of a specific task you do at work.

Now add the thought 'I am doing this for God.'

Here are some examples:

• 'Changing a nappy that floweth over . . .' for God.

• 'Answering the phone for the twenty third time in the last fifteen minutes . . .' for God.

• 'Writing a report on the attitudes of Kansas City housewives, aged 35–49, towards decaffeinated coffee in general and Maxwell House Decaffeinated in particular . . .' for God.

• 'Taking a difficult and slightly unpleasant client to lunch . . .' for God.

Caution: atheist at work

This call to good work I call the Nimrod Principle. Here's what Genesis 10:8–9 has to say:

> . . . Nimrod . . . grew to be a mighty warrior on

the earth. He was a mighty hunter before the Lord; that is why it is said, 'Like Nimrod a mighty hunter before the Lord.'

Two things strike me here. First, Nimrod was only a hunter but he gets his name into God's book because he was a 'mighty hunter'. Second, he did his hunting 'before the Lord'. In some way he felt himself account-able to God for the way he did his work. Think for a moment of your job and add the phrase 'before the Lord'.

Bryan – a mighty plumber – before the Lord.

Sarah – a mighty electrician – before the Lord.

Suppose for a moment you are wordprocessing a letter and you know that it is going to be sent to the Queen. You probably read it sixteen times before you print it out. And you print it out on the best paper you have. And then you think: 'Well, maybe if I just changed that word it might perhaps read slightly better. So you change it. Read it sixteen times. And print it out again. And check it again. How carefully we do our work is often determined by who we think is going to see it. Maybe the letter is not for the Queen or even the president of the company but that shouldn't make any difference.

Most of us are atheists when it comes to our work. We don't think God is looking.

'T' for ...?

One thing I've tried from time to time is to choose one job on my 'to do' list and dedicate it specifically to God, marking it with the letter 't' for task. It changes my attitude to that particular task and also to the other tasks on the list. That little 't' winks at me from the list

– a little reminder of the appropriate perspective for all my tasks. If only I used the 't' every day.

God is interested in excellence in everything we do. Joseph, Nehemiah and Daniel are three obvious examples of career success combined with outstanding service to God in a pagan environment. God seeks excellence and he rewards it. When he is looking for a craftsman to make the ark, the tent of meeting, and its furnishings, he tells Moses the particular individual he wants for the job – Bezalel. And he makes it quite clear which Bezalel he means:

> 'son of Uri, the son of Hur, of the tribe of Judah'
> *Exodus 31:2*

A man who is filled with his Spirit and 'with skill, ability and knowledge in all kinds of crafts' (31:3).

Similarly, when Solomon needs someone to do the bronzework in the temple no one within his own borders is good enough, and he has Huram, a man of mixed Israelite/Tyrian blood brought down from Tyre. Only the best will do.

Little big things

In Search of Excellence is one of the last decade's best-selling management books. Here's a quote from the introduction:

> 'For us, one of the main clues to corporate excellence has come to be just such incidents of unusual effort on the part of apparently ordinary individual employees.'
> *In Search of Excellence*, Peters & Waterman,
> Harper Collins, p.XVII

Great companies are made great not by stand-out individuals producing extraordinary work but by ordinary people going the extra mile, striving to do the basic things really well.

I was in the supermarket the other day. I got to the checkout and there was a young man there. He looked at me and said, 'Good afternoon, sir,' and smiled. 'Good afternoon,' I replied, already registering surprise. Normally I have to initiate any greeting with checkout people. He was fast, efficient, slightly formal.

'How would you like to pay, sir?'

No one ever calls me 'Sir'. Maybe I'm just getting old. But actually I liked it in his case – it was a mark of respect to a customer and it wasn't said coldly.

'Would you sign here?'

'Thank you.'

'Goodbye.'

Everything about the encounter was efficient, helpful and respectful. It was also unusual. Maybe doing the checkout is boring and I don't know how he was feeling. But I felt that I was an important and valued human being as I left the store with my milk and apples.

This kind of service is unusual. Some companies really do go for excellence but you might just as easily find yourself in a job where standards are quite low and morale poor. In such a situation, our standards remain God's, not our boss's or the company's. And, in fact, excellence can be infectious. Even a little bit of it. When one person starts doing things really well, it tends to generate two kinds of response – either resentment or a desire to do things equally well.

Avoiding the guilt trap

The call to excellent work, however, is not intended to burden us with false guilt about not being the best at whatever it is we do. The Bible clearly recognises different levels of ability. Bezalel is a craftsman of higher quality than Oholiab, the man God names as his No 2, and they, in turn, are presumably better than the other craftsmen whom God has, as he says, also given the ability to finish the work. Nevertheless, all are capable of work that is pleasing to God. In the parable of the talents, one man is given two talents. Another five. Both double their talents. Both make the most of what they have been given. God commends them both. Biblical success is making the most of what we have been given by God. It is not necessarily doing better than other people. This is an important distinction – we don't have to be the fastest bricklayer on the site, or in the town, or in the country, or in the world to please God.

Personal best?
Certainly, competition can be healthy. It can be a spur to improved performance. But competition can also be fuelled by envy, malice, greed, pride – a host of dark motivations that can embitter the individual, transform workplace relationships into a minefield of political intrigue and turn company rivalries sour and even criminal in the attempt to win.

Biblical success is not running faster than anyone else.

It is not just running the best time you can.

It is running the best time you can. With God's help.

We cannot do excellent work in an excellent way in our own strength. We can produce excellent work in our own strength. But not in a way that pleases God. Jesus is quite clear on this:

> 'I am the vine, you are the branches. Those who abide in me and I in them bear much fruit, because apart from me you can do nothing.'
> *John 15:5, NRSV*

Ultimately, Jesus is the equipper. And not just spiritually. David the warrior king records that it is God who trained his hands for war (Psalm 144:1). The writer to the Hebrews prays that Jesus, that great shepherd of the sheep, might equip the Hebrews with everything good for doing God's will (Hebrews 13:20).

It is through Christ that God equips us to do what is pleasing to him. As Le Roy Eims once said:

> 'The greatest way to maintain a spirit of excellence in our lives is an absolute yielding of our lives to the person of Jesus Christ himself.'

An extra mile?

It is not just that Jesus does all things well so that he becomes our example. It is also that he helps us to steer the course between two important and sometimes apparently conflicting ideas. The first comes out of this verse:

> 'So you also, when you have done everything that you were told to do, should say, "We are unworthy servants: we have only done our duty." '
>
> Luke 17:10

Is this not a call to go the extra mile? To do more than your job description requires and go above and beyond the call of duty? But what if our duty already requires sixty hours a week? Is there no end to the labour? And is this not in tension with Jesus' invitation:

> 'Come to me, all you who are weary and burdened, and I will give you rest. Take my yoke upon you and learn from me, for I am gentle and humble in heart, and you will find rest for your

souls. For my yoke is easy and my burden is light.'

Matthew 11:28–30

One of the ways to know how to respond to work demands is to go to Jesus. For many, excellence often has a devastatingly high price. It often only comes with hard work, late nights, dinners slowly turning to powder in the oven and, in many cases, divorce. It probably doesn't have to be that way. Work can become the great idol – and it is a voraciously hungry idol with an insatiable appetite for people's best time and best energies. If you are married the excuse that 'it's all for the family' may soon wear thin unless the family have been involved in the decision to make those kinds of sacrifices. The key is not just to ask Jesus how you can be excellent in your job but rather what kind of overall life will be most pleasing to God. The question is always: where does Jesus call you to follow him? And the answer he gives you, like the answer he gave to the apostle Peter or to the apostle John, will be for you alone, and may be totally different from the answer he gives to the Christian at the next desk.

In tough times, go to Jesus.

Sandy did.

She was organising a big corporate conference with senior executives flying in from all over the country. And travel plans and requirements in constant flux. She began to feel overwhelmed. That day God spoke to her in her quiet time. She was reading the story of the feeding of the five thousand. There seemed no way that Jesus could feed all the people but a young lad had five loaves and two fishes and made them available to Jesus. Jesus took what he brought and made it more than enough. On that day Sandy felt that God was saying to her: 'Bring to me what you have and I will supply the rest.'

In tough times when we are weary and strung out we can only bring what we have to God and ask him to supply the rest.

Excellence opens doors
Proverbs 22:29 says:

> Do you see a man skilled in his work?
> He will serve before kings;
> he will not serve before obscure men.

Nehemiah is a good example. He's cupbearer to the most powerful human on the planet. Artaxerxes, the Persian emperor. Cupbearing was an important job, entrusted to a senior official. The cupbearer was, after all, the last person to handle the wine before the emperor drank it. If you happened to be a fifth century emperor you chose your cupbearer very, very, very carefully. Artaxerxes had good reason to be wary – he had probably had to execute two of his brothers for rebellion. Nehemiah had made it to this top position even though he wasn't a Persian but an exiled Israelite, a member of a defeated and dispersed nation. It is the emperor's trust of Nehemiah and his personal concern for him that opens the door for Nehemiah to ask for the leave of absence and the resources to rebuild Jerusalem. And that concern is built on his job performance.

Our work is important to God in itself but it is also important as a component of our witness to our co-workers. We are at work to work. We are expected to produce good work. Work of one kind or another is what we produce. And we are viewed by people around us in the context of our work. Good work commands respect. Poor work, shoddy work, late work make it much harder to develop respect and therefore the kind of open relationship in which the gospel can be communicated. Good work can be a platform for ministry and evangelism but quite apart from that it is just downright satisfying to do something as well as you can.

Even cleaning ovenracks.

10

Who's the king of the castle?

Or relating to your boss

'I don't want any yes men around me. I want everybody to tell me the truth, even if it costs them their jobs.'

Samuel Goldwyn

SNAPSHOT

Pride comes before a fight

It's party time.

Our whole group is going out to celebrate a couple of promotions, to say thanks to some people moving to a different part of the company, to celebrate the boss's fortieth birthday, to build team morale. It's a welcome breather after a gruelling couple of months.

I go to a local bakery and buy a birthday cake big enough to feed twenty five, large and fluffy, and layered and peaked with cream. Later that evening we arrive at an elegant Italian restaurant, sip drinks, savour the antipasti, relish the main course. Good-natured banter bounces round the long table. We say 'well done' and 'thanks' and, as the large, fluffy, cream-dream arrives, 'happy birthday'. The cake is divided up and more good-natured banter bounces round the long table. Then my boss and the second-in-command, well-built sportsmen the pair, rise from their seats, a plate of fluffy, cream-topped cake in each hand. They come round the table and converge at my chair. They're standing over me. Good-naturedly they threaten the worst. Good-naturedly I do my best to feign a kind of Clint Eastwood cool. 'Go on,' I think to myself, 'make my day.'

Suddenly there's cake all over me. I'm out of my seat so fast it makes Lynford Christie look like a snail in wellies. With a surge of angry adrenalin I've pushed my boss, the birthday boy, caught him off balance and sent him across the room crashing onto a table and then onto the floor accompanied by a chair and some knives and forks. I am about to throw a punch at his second-in-command.

The Christian at work.

WHO'S THE BOSS?

Our relationship with our boss is often the most difficult relationship we have at work. It may not necessarily feel that way. In fact, many Christians I have talked to feel their relationship is just fine. But as we have explored the issue further God's word and spirit have often uncovered resentments and rebellions that we were previously unaware of. These resentments may sometimes rise from personality clashes or the perceived failings of the boss or indeed from the tensions caused by our own inadequate performance. At root, however, the problem in relating to our boss often comes from two sources.

First, pride – the difficulty most of us have in willingly and wholeheartedly submitting to anyone's authority. Few of us like to give up our independence. Few of us like to be in a situation where someone can say 'jump' and we have to. Most of us are in that situation.

Second, fear. At a time when millions of people are without paid work, our boss seems to wield even greater power – the power not only to deprive us of this job but to send us out into a marketplace where it may prove extremely difficult to find another one.

Furthermore, our contemporary understanding of the biblical concepts of fatherhood and love may be rather more romantic and cuddly than originally intended. Certainly, the father in the Bible is there to protect, provide and nurture, but he is also there to be obeyed. Similarly, Jesus emphasises the strong connection between love and obedience:

> 'If you love me, you will obey what I command.'
>
> *John 14:15*

> 'Whoever has my commands and obeys them, he is the one who loves me.'
>
> *John 14:21*

Love is inextricably connected to submission to authority.

Pride of place

On the whole Western culture has a problem with authority.

We respect the law less than we used to, we are suspicious of our politicians, we filter the media for moral and political bias, we accept our teachers' views more reluctantly than previous generations, we are more wary of the police than we used to be, and so on. Much of this suspicion is realistic and healthy. Authority is based on trust and if authority is abused then trust inevitably breaks down. The dangers of misused authority are clear and written large across the history of this and every preceding century. The Bible calls its leaders, whether political, religious, commercial or family, to use their God-given power in the service of others. Indeed, there is in the Bible a particular emphasis placed on the responsibility of the powerful to protect the powerless. The measure of the righteous king in the Old Testament is not how he treats his generals and landowners but how he treats the widow and the orphan and the alien – the vulnerable segments of the population. Similarly, the biblical legislation about employer/employee relations puts a heavy emphasis on justice and fair dealing.

It may not be our experience, but authority structures were intended for our benefit.

1 To help us grow in wisdom and character.

We can see this in the roles of parents, extended family, teachers and bosses. A good boss is a teacher – someone who helps us to develop skills, to anticipate and solve problems, to develop character traits that will enable us to do our job better and to overcome those weaknesses that affect our performance and working relationships.

2 To help protect us from destructive temptations.

A good boss protects his people from themselves and from the poor decisions and behaviours that might affect the business and them badly.

3 To help us receive direction for decisions.

A good boss sets and clarifies the overall direction, sets priorities and is a sounding board for decisions. A good boss also ensures his people have the resources to do the job.

This model of a good boss partially parallels the role of God's authority in our lives. Obedience to God's authority is for our benefit. In Eden, Adam failed to trust the truth of God's words and the reality of God's good intentions – God, he felt, was withholding something desirable from him and was protecting himself from having rivals. Adam failed to recognise his own limitations and thought he knew better. We all have our limitations. And we don't necessarily know best. We need to approach God and indeed those set in authority above us, with humility. Again they won't always be right – the world is full of corrupt companies and individuals – but our response to our boss should not spring from self-centredness, self-righteousness or selfish ambition but from a conscious awareness that his authority has been put into our lives with a benevolent purpose. And that purpose, like Joseph's unjust imprisonment by Potiphar, may not always be immediately apparent.

Fear of falling
Many of us believe that:
• The boss has authority.
• The boss has our future in her hands.
     But are these beliefs actually true?
     First, a startling biblical example.

Two great career opportunities?
Saul is king. David is not. David has been remarkably successful in all that Saul has asked him to do and Saul recognises that the Lord is with David and no longer with him. Saul sets out to try to thwart God's plan. As a result David, having already survived at least four assassination attempts, finds himself chased round Israel by Saul and his army. On two occasions at Engedi and again in Saul's field camp, David has a clear opportunity to kill Saul. Not unnaturally, David's men, who probably took no particular delight in being the objects of Saul's persistent and apparently vindictive pursuit, encourage him to do so. They see the opportunity as God-given. David does not kill the man in authority, nor will he allow anyone else to do his dirty work for him (1 Samuel 26:9). This has nothing to do with Saul's *behaviour* but everything to do with Saul's *status* before God. Saul is the Lord's anointed. The man placed in authority by God. David, unlike Saul, understands that the king's authority comes from God. Saul was not anointed king because he was the finest warrior, he was

made king because God chose him. But Saul cannot trust in that anointing enough to obey God. David, by contrast, has already been anointed by Samuel to be the next king but will not hasten his own coronation by raising his hand against the Lord's anointed. David is determined to wait for God's timing and God's means of installing him on the throne.

Authority from God

Saul's authority is from God. And David will flee from Saul but he will not seek to usurp that authority even though it is being so badly abused.

Another biblical example of submission to authority in action is Jesus before Pilate.

> 'Do you refuse to speak to me?' Pilate said. 'Don't you realise I have power either to free you or to crucify you?'
>
> Jesus answered, 'You would have no power over me, if it were not given you from above.'
>
> *John 19:10–11*

Jesus, the Son of God, has all power and authority but he submits to Pilate because of the authority Pilate has been given by God. Pilate is in fact misusing his authority. It is quite clear to him that Jesus is innocent of the charges against him but he allows himself to be manipulated by the Jewish leadership. Jesus points out not only that Pilate has received his authority from God and is accountable to him for its use but also that he, Jesus, is prepared to submit to Pilate's abuse of that power because that is God's will for him at that time.

The question is: do our secular bosses gain their authority from God?

Here's Paul in Romans:

Everyone must submit himself to the governing authorities, for there is no authority except that which God has established. The authorities that exist have been established by God. Consequently, he who rebels against the authority is rebelling against what God has instituted, and those who do so will bring judgement on themselves.

Romans 13:1–2

Paul is writing to the Christians in Rome and talking specifically about civil authority, a civil authority which many scholars believe had already grown unjustly hostile towards Christians. Nevertheless, Paul says 'submit'. Importantly, he does not argue from the specific circumstances of the situation but from a general principle, that there is no authority except from God.

Our boss's authority comes from God. That doesn't mean all her decisions do. Nor does it necessarily mean that Christians are never to be involved in overthrowing corrupt, tyrannical political regimes. It does mean, however, that unless some more important principle is being flouted, we are to obey our boss. A soldier is expected to obey a superior officer without question, but even within strict military discipline allowance is made for disobedience. There may be exceptions but it is important in developing the right attitude to recognise the general principle – we obey our boss primarily because we thereby obey God. That is we recognise that he has decreed that there should be structures of authority as a means of bringing order and justice to human relations. That doesn't mean we are to obey unwise decisions without question but it does mean we need to be careful before we challenge the person's authority.

In his letter to Titus Paul gives us another reason for obedience:

> 'Teach slaves to be subject to their masters in everything, to try to please them, not to talk back to them, and not to steal from them, but to show that they can be fully trusted, *so that in every way they will make the teaching about God our Saviour attractive.*'
>
> *Titus 2:9–10*

Our behaviour is meant to make the gospel attractive to those who are in authority over us – and our submission to them is perhaps understandably the first thing Paul points to. If someone doubts our basic acceptance of his right to direct then there really is no basis for a healthy working relationship.

Silence is golden ...

Mike Z was a Christian financial controller. A friendly, outgoing man who took a job working for a Jewish millionaire in a successful small business. To get to his boss's office Mike had to pass through an open-plan office area. As he did so he would say 'hello' to those who noticed him going through. It seemed the natural, friendly thing to do. His boss told him that he didn't want him talking to anyone on his way to his office. This seemed entirely unreasonable and somewhat cold and Mike continued to greet his co-workers.

His boss told him not to.

Mike prayed about the situation and decided to do what his boss told him rather than follow conventional working practice. A while later, his boss came up to him and said, 'You're a born-again Christian, aren't you?' Mike nodded, wondering what was coming. 'Well,' his boss continued, 'I'm looking to hire some more people. Know any of your kind who might be interested?' Mike's submission, as well as his general performance, had adorned the gospel. His employer wasn't yet a Christian but he recognised the difference Christ made in someone's life. And, to him at least, its commercial value.

Submission to human authority clearly has its limits – there is no call in Scripture to do things which are clearly immoral, illegal or against God's laws. The opposite is true. And this could cost a Christian his job. There is a need to look carefully at any problem situation and discern whether there are solutions which meet the boss's agenda and are still in line with God's laws. Daniel provides an excellent example.

Diet right – a diplomat's guide

Daniel, a young Israelite of significant intellectual and administrative promise, finds himself selected for training for the Babylonian civil service. He makes no objection to serving a pagan emperor in this way. He makes no objection to immersing himself in the 'language and literature of the Babylonians' (Daniel 1:4), literature that was predominantly idolatrous in orientation. Daniel makes no objection to being given a new name that commemorates the pagan deity Bel. In sum, Daniel is not a superspiritual individual who refuses to interact with the surrounding culture. There is, however, one area in which he resolves not to compromise – he will not consume the rich food and wine stipulated as the appropriate diet for budding civil servants. To Daniel that would have meant defiling himself.

Daniel's approach to the problem is respectful and highly creative. First, he asks permission of the official in charge of his wellbeing. Second, he takes the official's responsibilities and obligations into account. It is the official's job to keep the future imperial bureaucracy healthy. If he fails to do so, he may lose his job or his head. Daniel proposes a test – we'll eat vegetables and drink water for ten days and then you'll be able to see if we're sufficiently healthy to continue doing so. It was a test that acknowledged the official's concerns – long enough to show results but not so long as to endanger the connection between the official's head and his shoulder blades. A creative, negotiated solution where both sides won.

Whose employees are we anyway?

So we seek to obey our boss but not because we are slaves to men but because we are slaves of Christ:

> For he who was a slave when he was called by the Lord is the Lord's freedman; similarly, he who was a free man when he was called is Christ's slave. You were bought at a price; do not become slaves of men.'
>
> *1 Corinthians 7:22–23*

Our primary allegiance is to Christ. We serve him. One of the ways we do that is by serving our boss. The incentive for our service is not our boss's power but reverence for Christ:

> Slaves, obey your earthly masters in everything; and do it, not only when their eye is on you and to win their favour, but with sincerity of heart and *reverence for the Lord*.
>
> *Colossians 3:22*

This is a radical call and Paul reinforces it in the following two verses:

> Whatever you do, work at it with all your heart,

as working for the Lord, not for men, since you
know that you will receive an inheritance from
the Lord as a reward. It is the Lord Christ you
are serving.

So when you work the extra hours and no one notices
do you consider that you will receive an inheritance
from the Lord as a reward?

And when your boss asks you to do something, do
you see Christ standing behind her saying, 'Do it for
me.' Or do you resent her, and perhaps sometimes even
go so far as to blame all the frustration of a particular
task – the rain and the mud and the equipment that
hasn't arrived and the short tempers of the rest of the
team – on the boss who gave you the task in the first
place?

Future block?
The second reason that many of us feel tension with
our boss is that we believe that she has our destiny
in our hands. She decides whether I get a pay rise,
whether I keep my job, whether I get promoted.

Is that true?

Psalm 93:1 begins: 'The Lord reigns'. Indeed, the
ultimate sovereignty of God is a consistent theme
throughout the Bible. But does he reign over my career
prospects?

The Bible makes it clear that God is in control of our
bosses. He may not always choose to exercise that
power but he can:

The king's heart is in the hand of the Lord;
he directs it like a watercourse wherever he
pleases.

Proverbs 21:1

And God may well use that sovereign power for your benefit. Just as he used the Babylonians to accomplish his purposes in the people of Israel so he may use your boss to accomplish his purposes in you. He is sovereign and he loves you, and all things work together for good to those who love him, and are called according to his purpose. This has some startling implications. If God is sovereign and wants the best for you then the boss you have is the boss God wants you to have. The boss you have is the perfect boss for you right now. God is a teacher and he is using that person in your life to teach you.

The question is what does he want to teach you?

What are you meant to be learning?

BOSS – tailor-made?
Your boss is not an unfortunate obstacle in your path to spiritual maturity but far more likely to be an instrument in God's hand to bring about that spiritual maturity.

God is in control of our bosses. And he is in control even when they have lost control, when circumstances arise in which they are unable to act on our behalf even though they might want to.

Again Daniel's life provides an example of an employee whose boss has completely lost control of a situation. Daniel is working for Darius, the third emperor he has served, and he has done such an outstanding job that Darius plans, as we saw earlier, to make him chief administrator of the entire empire. The plan provokes Daniel's colleagues to try to find a way to discredit him. Finding no fault in his performance or morality they are forced to devise a scheme to discredit him through his faith in the God of Israel. They persuade the king to sign a decree that anyone who prays to any god or man except the king for the following thirty days should be thrown into the lions' den.

Daniel refuses to comply with the edict. His colleagues report the matter to the king, reminding him of the inviolability of the law – not even he can repeal a law once given. Reluctantly the king consigns Daniel to the lions but with the sincere wish: 'May your God, whom you serve continually, rescue you.' That night the king fasts.

Darius has lost control of the situation. He finds himself, even as emperor, unable to protect his employee. God, however, is able and intervenes decisively.

The belief that our boss has our future in her hands stands in direct contradiction to the Bible. Our future is in fact determined by:

1 God's plan for our lives.
2 Our response to God as the plan unfolds.

Moses is a murderer with limited public-speaking skills. He is also an experienced shepherd with a tremendous love for his people. Most importantly, however, he responds to God's revelation of himself and to his commands. And he becomes leader of the people of Israel.

Daniel begins as just one of a group of young Israelite scholars. And becomes chief administrator.

David is just a young shepherd, indeed the youngest son in a large family. And he becomes king of Israel.

God is in charge:

> For neither from the east nor from the west, nor from the desert does promotion come; but God is the judge. He puts one down and promotes another.
>
> *Psalm 75:6–7, New Berkeley Version*

The way to 'up' is sometimes down

As far as promotion is concerned I have had my ups and downs. On one occasion I was promised an early promotion, but for reasons beyond my immediate boss's control it kept on being delayed. I felt jerked around, lost perspective and started to become resentful. Instead of enjoying the fact that I was going to be given new responsibilities in due course I became focused on my promotion happening as soon as possible. It began to occupy far too much of my thinking time, probably adversely affecting my performance. Why was I so anxious? So wound up? Was it lust for recognition? Quite probably.

On another occasion four people of roughly similar experience were promoted and I wasn't. I was pretty upset but I soon realised that I wasn't actually terribly interested in doing the next job up at that time and that I was simply suffering from wounded pride. Soon afterwards I was asked to co-direct the training programme – an experience of immense joy that I would have missed had I been promoted earlier.

On a third occasion, however, I was furious. I had recently had a stellar evaluation from my immediate boss. She had told me, and I jest not, that I 'could become a giant in the industry, if I wanted to.' A few weeks later six people got promoted and I didn't. If I was a giant how come I was being treated like a dwarf? Hell hath no fury like a woman, or an adman, scorned. My anger seethed like a volcano on the brink of explosion, erupting late at night in long soliloquies addressed to my bedroom ceiling. Impassioned paragraphs of measured, invincible logic on the facts of the matter, my own galactic achievements, the Machiaevellian machinations that had lead to this miscarriage of justice, the vacuum of discernment that had precipitated this ignominious betrayal of talent and loyalty, the weakness of character that had led to this pathetic pandering to the squeaking wheedlers oiling their way up the ladder of power. I had, in my view, been stabbed in the back.

I thought angry thoughts to God: 'I trusted you. I gave you my career. Now look what a mess you've made of it.' But he was there. At the train station, the ticket-seller responded to my offer of a tract with a pat on the hand and some kind words; the very evening of the catastrophe when I arrived home and forced myself resentfully to open my Bible the first words that I saw were from Psalm 37: 'Fret not'. Like a father to an overwrought child.

Don't be anxious.

It made me laugh and put things into some kind of perspective, temporarily at least. It had been easy to memorise the verse about God exalting one and putting down another. It turned out to be much harder to apply it. Through that experience, however, I became wiser. God taught me that I had been somewhat naive, that I had failed to manage my career, failed to communicate to those above me where I wanted to go. I had seen the company as a benevolent parent who would always be fair, rather than as an inevitably flawed group of people doing their best to juggle the interests of the company with the interests of their clients with the interests of individual employees. And besides, I had to ask myself the question: is someone who doesn't know how to manage senior people within the company the right person to interact with senior clients?

I saw the company as a benevolent parent partly because of the way that I tend to respond to authority. I am inclined, except when covered with cake, to avoid disagreement and to bottle up feelings of anger. At its worst this tendency can lead to a failure to contradict the boss even when you know what he is proposing is downright wrong. Conversely, more independent types may overreact in the opposite direction and see the boss as the enemy and secretly or openly rebel against any limitation of their independence. Neither is healthy.

No guarantees

In my case, other opportunities for promotion came – but they might not have. God looks after his own. God does honour those who honour him but there is absolutely no guarantee of success, no guarantee that we won't be fired or passed over. We can never take his grace for granted. The call is always to follow him. Whether to a painful death on a cross, like the apostle Peter, or like many Sudanese Christians in the last few years. Or to a long life, like the disciple John, or like Billy Graham.

The conviction that God is the boss is, in fact, liberating. Faced by an intensely irritating manager or an impulsive, tyrannical foreman we can ask ourselves, how is my real boss treating me?

Looking after number two?

At one point I had a boss who was, I felt, lazy, unreasonable, untalented, a creative craftsman of the truth, a glory seeker and a chauvinist. I was, you might say, 'uncomfortable with his management style'. At least that's how I saw it at the time.

Suddenly, two thoughts struck me. First, I put my boss in perspective. OK, this man is not treating me that well, or at least so I thought, but how is my real boss treating me? Apart from dying for me and sending me the Holy Spirit. And blessing me with a good church. And giving me a fine pastor and a marvellous discipler. And a lovely family. And great friends. And a nice place to live. In an exciting city. And, on the whole, great people to work with. Not to mention health and food and pots of money. In fact, my real boss was really being lavish in his generosity. And the relationship with my boss, though significant, was a tiny puff of cloud in an ocean of azure sky.

The second thought that struck me was this: this lazy, unreasonable, Machiaevellian office politician, this creative craftsman of the truth, this glory-seeking chauvinist is someone that God loves. How could that be? Jesus died for this person. Was I even praying for him?

And was I giving him a chance?

I've been on the business a year and know the clients well and am liked and respected. Then he comes in. Do I really support him? Help him to learn the business?

The result of my lack of support for him might well be that when I have a problem that I can't resolve and I really need someone higher up, I have so undermined my boss that he doesn't have the credibility with the clients to help me.

Which one of us is the jerk really?

I hadn't taken the time to teach him the business. I hadn't considered his insecurity in a new and demanding role. And I wasn't prepared to let go of my status to help him establish himself. I was focused on looking good myself rather than on making him look good. On looking good myself rather than on doing what was best for the business. I was too focused on looking after number one to remember that I was actually meant to be number two.

Furthermore, I didn't think about his strengths, didn't think about how to improve the way we worked together, didn't think about how to make our different workstyles as productive as possible for the business. Furthermore, I wasn't prepared to tell him the problems that I had with him. He might not have been a great boss but I wasn't doing too well being the perfect subordinate.

A servant heart would not have shown up in an autopsy.

So, although I thought that I was the innocent party I had made a significant contribution to the problem. Certainly, we got on quite well but underneath the surface jollity lurked a bubbling sea of resentments that I was hardly aware of and was almost certainly unwilling to admit to myself. The bottom line was that I had certainly not treated him with anything like authentic love.

Blueprint for the radical employee

The biblical model for both the employer and the employee is that of a servant – one who deploys his gifts and resources for the benefit of another person. And Christ is the supreme example of that. It is he we must seek to imitate:

> Be imitators of God, therefore, as dearly loved children, and live a life of love, just as Christ loved us and gave himself up for us as a fragrant offering and sacrifice to God.
>
> *Ephesians 5:1–2*

Christ consistently recognised God's authority – and he acts in line with his Father's will:

> 'I tell you the truth, the Son can do nothing by himself; he can do only what he sees his Father

doing, because whatever the Father does the Son also does.'

John 5:19

Jesus' teaching is not his own but 'comes from him who sent me' (John 7:16); he does not seek glory for himself (John 8:50) but gives God the credit, and gains his reward and significance from God.

Bricks without straw?

Christ calls us to go one step further in our relationship with our employers:

'So you also when you have done everything that you were told to do, should say, "We are unworthy servants; we have only done our duty." '

Luke 17:10

This is not a mandate for longer hours, for the workaholism that plagues some people or for acceptance of the crushing pressure that some companies bring to bear on their employees, but rather a summons to a willing, thoughtful attitude. As Paul writes in another context, 'The Lord loves a cheerful giver.' The true servant is not simply looking to fulfil his obligations but to *serve*, to be looking out for ways of helping his employer, to make her job easier.

One of the keys to working well with our boss is to know their expectations and to understand their preferred way of working. And to adapt accordingly. Some bosses like a lot of information, some don't like much. Some like written reports and recommendations, some prefer discussion. Some are very much hands-on, some are delegators. Know your boss. This has nothing to do with political manoeuvring but everything to do with getting the job done as efficiently as possible. As Gabarro and Kotter pointed out in the Harvard Business Review in 1979, knowing how to manage upwards is a vital part of getting the job done well. You and your boss are in a relationship. You are both fallible. You both need each other. Work at getting it right.

Is your relationship with your boss creative and dynamic? Do you love your boss as yourself? Pray for her? Do you deal creatively and courageously with the things she does that bother you? Do you support her? Do you recognise your responsibility to submit to her authority even though you may need to challenge some of her decisions? Do you know her expectations? Do you seek to work out ways to make your working relationship as productive as possible? Do you believe that it is God who is in charge of your career and that he will use your workplace and your boss to accomplish his purposes in your life?

Quite often I didn't.

E P I L O G U E

Fighting Back?

It was the morning after the night before.

I'd got most of the cream off my suit. The dry cleaners would do the rest. There had been several phone calls from people who worked with me and there hadn't been much sleep. Now it was time to go to work.

I knew what I was supposed to do.

I knew what I had to do.

I had to get in early and go and see my boss – at least the one I'd propelled across a restaurant in front of his staff – and I had to apologise. I had no idea how he would react. Understandably he had been angry the night before when we talked outside the restaurant. Even more understandably since he, in fact, hadn't contributed any of his birthday cake to my suit.

I knocked on his door. He said, 'Come in,' and turned round from his desk to face me. I could see the tension in his face. I sat down opposite him and apologised and said that there was no excuse for the way I had reacted. I could see the tension disappear from his face. He accepted my apology without reproving me at all and said that that was the end of the matter.

It was.

He never mentioned it again.

He treated me just as fairly and firmly and generously as he had before.

Indeed, after he left the agency to work elsewhere he twice called me up to offer me a job in his new company.

It remains one of the most startling incidents of forgiveness I have ever experienced.

11

Rebel, rebel?
Or no hard feelings?

'How can you say to your brother, "Let me take the speck out of your eye," when all the time there is a plank in your own eye?'
Matthew 7:4

A PAUSE FOR THOUGHT

This chapter is, if you like, a time for you to pause and reflect on some of your attitudes to authority in general and to your boss in particular. I've found in seminars that I've taught that this exercise is both helpful and sometimes surprising for people. You may discover attitudes that you never knew were there. And sometimes even attitudes that you definitely thought were *not* there.

For the most part this chapter contains verses from Scripture, unadorned by commentary. Read them slowly perhaps and see if the Holy Spirit brings something to mind as you consider for yourself how these verses might apply to you:

1 Our boss's authority is from God and we are to submit to it:

> Everyone must submit himself to the governing authorities, for there is no authority except that which God has established. The authorities that exist have been established by God.
>
> *Romans 13:1*

2 We submit to our boss's authority to adorn the Good News:

> Teach slaves to be subject to their masters in everything, to try to please them, not to talk back to them, and not to steal from them, but to show that they can be fully trusted, so that in every

way they will make the teaching about God our Saviour attractive.

Titus 2:9, 10

3 God is our real boss:

Whatever you do, work at it with all your heart, as working for the Lord, not for men, since you know that you will receive an inheritance from the Lord as a reward. It is the Lord Christ you are serving.

Colossians 3:23, 24

4 God is in control of our careers, promotions, success and failure:

For neither from the east, nor from the west, nor from the desert does promotion come; but God is the judge. He puts down one and promotes another.

Psalm 75:6, 7, New Berkeley Version

5 God loves your boss:

'For God so loved the world that he gave his one and only Son, that whoever believes in him shall not perish but have eternal life.'

John 3:16

6 We should not criticize our boss publicly or encourage complaints.

An example: Absalom's public criticism of David in 2 Samuel 15:1–6.

The situation: Absalom, harbouring anger against David, spends four years standing by the road on the way up to the city, ingratiating himself with passers-by and promising them 'favourable' justice – if only he were appointed judge in the land.

Of course, if I were in charge of this business, all would be well . . .

7 We owe our boss outward and heart-felt loyalty regardless of whether it's beneficial to us in the short-term.

An example: Ittai the Gittite, 2 Samuel 15:14ff.

The situation: Absalom, King David's own son, has, after years of trying to undermine David's authority, finally rebelled openly. David is forced to flee from Jerusalem. Ittai the Gittite and his 600 men are with him. Ittai is not an Israelite, he has no binding obligation to stand with David against Absalom, and he arrived in Jerusalem only the day before the rebellion broke out. Furthermore, David has expressly released him from any duty to go with him. But Ittai has made a commitment to David. It's a commitment that may well result in his death but it's one that he sticks by:

> 'As surely as the Lord lives, and as my lord the king lives, wherever my lord the king may be, whether it means life or death, there will your servant be.'
>
> *2 Samuel 15:21*

This is loyalty. And though the circumstances are almost too extreme to find contemporary comparisons, what level of loyalty do you feel towards your boss?

8 We need to make sure we have flushed out any unresolved anger, resentments or negative feelings. They lead to cake on the suit or perhaps a spear in the wall.

To some significant extent I may well have been harbouring unconfessed resentment towards those in authority above me, which contributed to the intensity of my response to having sponge cake daubed over my suit.

Get rid of all bitterness, rage and anger, brawling and slander, along with every form of malice.

Ephesians 4:31

9 Some questions to ask. Some verses to consider:
- Am I selfishly ambitious?

For where you have envy and selfish ambition, there you find disorder and every evil practice.

James 3:16

- Am I really considering my boss's needs?

Do nothing out of selfish ambition or vain conceit, but in humility consider others better than yourselves. Each of you should look not only to your own interests, but also to the interests of others.

Philippians 2:3, 4

- Am I trying to take the credit?

For it is not the man who commends himself who is approved, but the man whom the Lord commends.

2 Corinthians 10:18
(see also *Luke 14:7–11*)

- Am I proud?

'To fear the Lord is to hate evil:
I hate pride and arrogance,
evil behaviour and perverse speech.'

Proverbs 8:13

- Am I really submitting to my boss's authority? Or simply doing what I'm told?

Teach slaves to be subject to their masters in

everything, to try to please them, not to talk back
to them . . .'

Titus 2:9

• Do I genuinely forgive my boss when he does something wrong?

> Be kind and compassionate to one another, forgiving each other, just as in Christ God forgave you.
>
> *Ephesians 4:32*
> (see also *Matthew 18:21, 22*)

• Do I love my boss and actively seek opportunities to express that love?

> Dear children, let us not love with words or tongue but with actions and in truth.
>
> *1 John 3:18*

• Do I fail to see the opportunities in apparently adverse circumstances?

> Count it pure joy, my brothers, whenever you face trials of many kinds, because you know that the testing of your faith develops perseverance.
>
> *James 1:2, 3*

> Now I want you to know, brothers, that what has happened to me has really served to advance the gospel. As a result, it has become clear throughout the whole palace guard and to everyone else that I am in chains for Christ. Because of my chains, most of the brothers in the Lord have been encouraged to speak the word of God more courageously and fearlessly.
>
> *Philippians 1:12–14*

• Do I communicate my problems with my boss to him?

And do I do it lovingly?

> Instead, speaking the truth in love, we will in all things grow up into him who is the head, that is, Christ.
>
> *Ephesians 4:15*

What discoveries have you made?

> If we confess our sins,
> he is
> faithful and just
> and
> will forgive us our sins
> and
> purify us
> from all unrighteousness.
>
> *1 John 1:9*

12

When the heat is on
Or business as usual?

'O Lord, who may abide in your tent?
Who may dwell on your holy hill?
Those who walk blamelessly, and do what is
right . . .'

Psalm 15: 1–2 NRSV

WHEN THE HEAT IS ON

Work is not morally neutral.

It is either conducted in a manner that is in line with God's word, or it isn't. Every job has different kinds of ethical issues and every business is full of people making decisions about how to conduct that business. Here are three true case studies that may help you consider some of the issues involved in being a Christian in your workplace. The people involved faced quite different challenges and dealt with them as they thought best at the time. Were they right or wrong? What would you have done?

CASE STUDY 1

Should Carol sing?
Or tax and how to avoid it?

Let's call her Carol, a 21 year old trainee accountant, shy to the point of being deferential to supersoft teddy bears. She'd been working in a small accountancy firm for about a year. One afternoon she was asked by her boss to put non-existent expenses on to a client's VAT return. This would mean that the client would pay less VAT than legally required.

At the same time Carol knew that the firm were putting non-existent employees' salaries on to the client's pay-roll. Which meant that the non-existent salaries could actually be paid to senior clients without those senior clients incurring a higher rate of income tax.

The senior partners in the firm were both Christians and knew what was going on.

• What would you do?

• What are the likely consequences of any action Carol takes?

What happened

Carol refused to do what her boss told her to. He said, 'I could fire you.' She said, 'Fine.' And he put the non-existent receipts on the VAT return himself.

This left Carol with another moral dilemma.

Should she report the manager to one of the partners, both of whom were Christians? Although they did in fact know what was happening.

Should she confront them with their illegal and ungodly conduct?

Should she report the matter to the police or the Inland Revenue?

None of them easy options for someone who is deferential to supersoft teddy bears.

In fact, at the time, Carol didn't have the confidence to go to the authorities. She let the matter drop. She hoped that her own stand would speak to the manager and to her bosses. Five years on, and with the confidence to take on a charging Canadian grizzly with a matchstick she still believes that it was the right thing to do at the time.

CASE STUDY 2

The cost of honesty?

When Michael became a Christian he had five girlfriends, two mortgages, a pile of debt and a thriving picture-framing business.

First to go were four of the girlfriends, leaving Lise, the Christian woman he'd known for three weeks who'd lead him to Christ. But he still had two mortgages and a pile of debt. He also discovered that he had a nagging conscience, telling him that he really ought to have registered for VAT and fully disclosed his income. He hadn't been registered for VAT or taxed on his full income for seven years. He would have to pay a lot of money. And that would massively increase his debt.

Michael went to an accountant for advice. The accountant told him that the best thing to do would be to say nothing to the Inland Revenue and simply close down the current business and open up a new one in a new location. That way, all back tax and VAT would be neatly avoided. The Inland Revenue would never know. Sensible advice. But also illegal.

• What would you do?

What happened

Michael decided to come clean. To register for VAT and fully disclose his prior income. It put him under immense pressure financially. He also decided to register his employee for national insurance, even though the employee was happy to continue with the prior arrangement. His friends tried to dissuade him. When he went to buy materials for his shop he was encouraged by the salespeople not to pay the VAT. 'Nobody else does.' 'You're a mug mate.' Michael paid it. On one occasion the shopkeeper simply pocketed the money himself and didn't register the purchase for VAT.

Michael's turnover, though healthy, was not high enough to service all his debt. He went bankrupt. And there was a risk that Lise, now his wife, might have to give up her course at Bible college.

But somehow there's always been enough money – just.

Lise reacted this way, 'It's like that occasion in John's Gospel when a lot of people have left Jesus and he turns to Peter and says, "Are you leaving too?" Peter says, "Where shall I go? You have the words of eternal life." There's nothing else for us to do. You can live dishonestly as a Christian and have uncomfortable feelings but you know you're going to be accountable for it in the long run.

'We know we've done the right thing, even though it's been like being squeezed through the eye of a needle.'

Michael is still in the picture-framing business.

His landlord has allowed him to stay rent free until there's another tenant.

CASE STUDY 3

To copy or not to copy?

Diane is a secretary in a London company. A friend of hers asks her to do a small amount of private photocopying for him. At first she agrees, but then she begins to have second thoughts. She knows that there would be no point in paying for it – the accounts department wouldn't know what to do with such a small sum.

- What would you do?

What happened

Diane decided that she would simply be taking advantage of the goodwill of her company if she photocopied the material and she refused to do it. She returned the originals to her friend. He accused her of hypocrisy, saying that she had never been so strict about such matters before. She replied, 'I've got to start somewhere.'

Big things, little things – we've all got to start somewhere.

13

You're the boss too?

Question: What, apart from giving you a payrise every six months, are the characteristics of a good boss?
Answer: 'Ears.'
Roger Howe, Maintenance Officer

'O! It is excellent to have a giant's strength, but it is tyrannous to use it like a giant.'
William Shakespeare

REVENGE IS SWEET

Recently my secretary acquired a new toy. It's a doll about fifteen inches high. He has a corporate look about him – pinstriped trousers, and matching tie and braces. There's a whip in one hand and a Churchillian cigar in the other and he's wearing a badge which says, 'Because I'm the **BOSS**'. He has a severe, somewhat maniacal look about his beady-eyed face and one of his employees is hanging by his trousers from his capacious jaws. Interestingly, his limbs and his head are attached to his body with Velcro. When you're stressed out with your real boss you're supposed to rip this little fellow limb from limb and head from torso. And throw the pieces against a wall. Or maybe stamp on them.

I don't know why my secretary has acquired this toy.

He has brown eyes like me. And dark hair like me. But he has no beard and his nose is no rival to Concorde. Must be the other guy my secretary works for.

The stereotypical image of the boss is of the one we love to hate – a paragon of unreason, impossible demands, contradictory instructions, bad jokes guffawed at with counterfeit glee. Still, an awful lot of us have people working for us. An awful lot of us are bosses. Are we like that?

I don't know if I'm a good boss. I do know that when I asked people in my workplace to quickly jot down a few words about the characteristics of a good boss, no one wrote back, 'Look in the mirror, sweet angel'.

I wonder what you think are the characteristics of a good boss.

Here are some of the things my colleagues wrote:

• Listens to his staff. Is impartial between staff. Makes decisions that are considered, wise and reliable. Is able to do the hard things fairly and firmly.

• Knows where she wants the organisation to go, tells me, helps me to help her get there, and thanks me on arrival.

• Willing to listen, cooperative, decision-making, analytical, clear, resilient.

• Hardworking, trustful, thoughtful.

• Shows respect. Is interested in my personal welfare (other than to do with work), a good listener, takes my comments and suggestions seriously, gives feedback.

• Communicates, delegates, doesn't interfere in one's work or correct employees in front of others, has a sense of humour, treats one as an intelligent being.

• Sticks up for his employees. Leads by example. Is pastorally concerned but wields a heavy hand when necessary. Asks the right person to do the right job.

• Lets you get on with your work but doesn't mind if you come running when it all goes horribly wrong. Is patient, has a sense of humour. Much the same as a good husband really. Though he doesn't have to be at least six foot tall, have straight teeth and be able to sing in tune. (Applications, preferably with a photo to . . .)

• Encourages. Is occasionally appreciative, considerate, well-mannered. Delegates. Is completely open about the work and his expectations.

• Listens to ideas/points of view. Delegates responsibility. Allows a person to use his initiative. Is approachable. Is for a person's development.

- Cares about me and knows his job.

The business of leading and managing people has become a big business all of its own. Airport and train station bookshops are full of books about it, intended to lure busy bosses (at least the ones who don't have laptop computers) into using their travel time to improve job performance, managerial skills, career progress and, of course, that most insistent of taskmasters – the bottom line. Offering advice gleaned from the Japanese, from what Harvard Business School doesn't teach, from dolphins and Attila the Hun, and from more benign leaders like John Harvey Jones and Lee Iacocca.

It's not my intention to evaluate the whole gamut of material on offer, nor to look at how to improve particular management skills. Rather I'd like to focus on a small number of biblical principles.

If you look at my colleagues' responses again you'll see they could be broken down into four main areas:

Vision and direction Someone who knows where he's going and what he wants done – knows the task and can set direction.

Competence Someone who can do her own job and can help me do mine.

Integrity Someone to look up to – a person of integrity, who is hardworking, trustworthy, honest, open, loyal, fair.

Love Someone who listens, respects, is concerned for his employees, has a sense of humour, can build a team.

Of these the last one – love – is perhaps the most startling and the one that you're unlikely to find in many management textbooks. Though, to be fair, you will find many of its manifestations – listening, developing, etc. There is, however, a critical difference. The Christian boss behaves in certain ways not because they will affect the bottom line but because those ways are consistent with what God has to say about dealing with people. The Christian boss doesn't simply respect his employees because employees who feel respected work better, faster and more cost-effectively but because the Bible says that people are infinitely valuable. The Christian boss is concerned for her employees as people, rather than as cogs in the company machine, and she is concerned for them not just because happy, healthy, stable people work better, faster, cheaper but because people are always more than they do, more than the functions they perform at work. The guiding principles for good management must at root be *theological* ideas, derived from the character of God, the example of Christ and the words of scripture.

The servant boss

Three linked ideas seem to dominate what God is looking for in a leader. A clue to the first is in Solomon's prayer at the beginning of his reign:

> 'Now, O Lord my God, you have made your servant king in place of my father David. But I am only a little child and do not know how to carry out my duties. Your servant is here among the people you have chosen, a great people, too numerous to count or number. So give your servant a discerning heart to govern your people and to distinguish between right and wrong. For who is able to govern this great people of yours?'
>
> The Lord was pleased that Solomon had asked for this. So God said to him, 'Since you have asked for this and not for long life or wealth for yourself, nor have asked for the death of your enemies but for discernment in administering

> justice, I will do what you have asked. I will give you a wise and discerning heart, so that there will never have been anyone like you, nor will there ever be.'
>
> *1 Kings 3:7–12*

God's pleasure does not stem from the fact that Solomon asks for wisdom in itself. It stems from the fact that he asks for wisdom for a particular purpose – so that he can govern God's people and do it justly. The wisdom he seeks is not primarily for himself but for the people he is going to govern. His desire is selfless. And it is contrasted with a set of desires that would have been selfish – wealth, long life, security from his enemies. In contemporary terms – a fat annual bonus, a fabulous pension package and the demise of all serious competitors for his job and his company's customers. It is wisdom put at the service of others. The motive is love for God's people as well as a keen sense of personal inadequacy for the task ahead. God gives us gifts not just for ourselves but to serve others. The Christian boss, manager, leader is always a servant. Obviously he still exercises authority and power, just as Jesus did, but he does so with other people's interests at heart:

> Do nothing out of selfish ambition or vain conceit, but in humility consider others better than yourselves. Each of you should look not only to your own interests, but also to the interests of others.
>
> *Philippians 2:3–4*

How far do you have your people's interests at heart? Are you a servant leader?

Are you concerned about your people's development or only concerned about the extent to which they can contribute to your advancement?

Do you want them to grow? As people as well as operators? Do you pray for wisdom and discernment in helping them develop? Are you honest with them about their prospects for advancement and rewards?

And how do you regard those in the company who do apparently less important work?

Uncommon courtesy

David Warden is a Christian ad executive. He left one agency to join another. His former president wanted him to come back. He was not only a first class ad executive but, she had come to realise, the most 'loved' man at his old agency. He made a huge difference to morale. In his new company, a secretary was introduced to him. She said, 'Oh, you're David Warden. You're the one who says 'hello' to receptionists. I've been dying to meet you.' Simple, common courtesy. Treating people with respect, whatever their rank. And so rare in the corporate world as to be noteworthy. No wonder people love David. No wonder people love to *work* for David. He treats them with love.

God is love. But that doesn't make him soft or ill-disciplined or tolerant of slapdash mediocrity. Skills and standards are important – not just in themselves but for the impact they have on people. You don't love people by circulating poorly constructed, vague, overfull agendas. You don't love people by delegating work to them which they have neither the skills nor the resources to accomplish. You don't love people by putting off telling them that there are areas of their job performance which are inadequate just because you will find the conversation uncomfortable. Firing them will be a lot more uncomfortable.

Justice

The second criterion is justice. The good boss is a just judge. Rewarding people according to merit and effort. Promoting those with the skills for the job, not those who know how to ingratiate themselves with their superiors. Very few things are more corrosive in an organisation than the sense that politics or the application of emotional pressure will be rewarded more highly than merit. It rankles in every heart and tends to make many people spend more time working out how to look great than working out how to do work that's great.

Justice also has a bearing on protection. Interestingly, as I have mentioned, the righteous king in Psalm 72 is not evaluated by the way he treats his generals and high priests and chief administrators but by the way he administers the law to those who had no power before the law:

> 'He will defend the afflicted among the people
> and save the children of the needy,
> he will crush the oppressor.'
>
> *Psalm 72:4*

Elsewhere there's an emphasis on defending the alien, the widow, the orphan – people with no one to intercede for them.

The measure of a good leader is not how she treats the people she needs – but how she treats the people who are less important and have no apparent, direct bearing on her advancement. In God's field of vision the 'little people' loom large. How do you treat them?

Bringing out the best

The third quality is genuine care for the people who work for you as people. The righteous king in the

Old Testament is also the caring shepherd – providing, nurturing, protecting, developing. Again, this has nothing to do with being soft on poor performance or losing sight of the task to be accomplished but everything to do with helping people do their best, give their best, be their best. And that is going to change from individual to individual. The good boss treats everyone fairly but doesn't treat everyone the same.

One of my bosses used to say to me, 'If you buy a dog, don't bark yourself.' I was the dog. It was my job to bark. He gave me clear overall direction, clear goals, but a lot of leash on how to reach them. Freedom for initiative. And a genuine sense of responsibility. It was just right for me at that time. At other stages of my career he might have responded differently. I would have needed a lot of supervision, a lot of teaching. The key to being a good boss is being able to discern how to be there for people at the different stages of their development – offering help, or leaving the door open, or showing someone how to do something.

This goes beyond simply recognising what advice and/or resources they need to get the job done well but extends to their personality needs. Take, for example, a woman who has just finished some very important work that is going to be shown to a client the next day. She goes into her male boss and says joyfully, 'It's done. Would you like to see it before the meeting?' He trusts her and knows that she's good at what she does. He is a 'new man' and doesn't want to patronise his female subordinate in any way. In fact, he wants to affirm her, so he says, 'No, thanks. I'll see it at the meeting. I'm sure it's great.' She leaves the room disappointed, thinking that he doesn't really care. It wasn't the right way to handle her. And, though I'm now entering the minefield of gender differences here, research does suggest that it might not have been the right way to handle many women in that situation, although it might have been the right way to handle a lot of men. The point here is not to get into a discussion of the different ways that men and women communicate and prefer to be communicated with but simply to make the crushingly obvious but vital point that we can never apply a simple formula to people. The good shepherd knows his sheep by name.

The good shepherd helps his people to grow. This can sometimes mean encouraging them to look for different work or work elsewhere. Not so long ago I had someone reporting to me who worked hard, was smart and apparently competent but didn't really pro-duce the results. Week by week I would try to show him how to do this particular job. Finally, I came to two conclusions. First: this person was in the wrong job and should leave. Second: I would in all honesty be able to give him an excellent reference for the right job. It was simply a case of being a square peg in a round hole. I summoned up my courage to talk to him about it at our weekly update meeting. He walked into my office and, before I could say anything, told me that he had come to the conclusion that the job simply wasn't him and that he would like to leave. He hadn't been particularly happy and he had the wisdom to see his situation clearly and to do something about it. But he might not have, and we don't do anyone any favours by leaving them in jobs that they don't do well and that don't really suit them.

The good shepherd looks after his people as people. Fights for better working conditions. Proper training. Fair rewards. And the right perspectives about the place of work in people's lives.

Life before work?

A while back Tony had a heart attack.

It was his second.

He's a senior financial services salesman with a role in the office and a role on the road. A lot of pressure. He's married and has two children. His doctor told him to take it easy. His manager, Gerry, is a Christian and he went to see Tony in hospital. Gerry suggested that he take a disability pension or come back part-time. Less money, to be sure. But less pressure. Tony wasn't too thrilled. He wanted his old job back. And, in a sense, he had a right to it. Gerry pointed out that maybe his family would rather live slightly less well and have him alive than have an empty place at the table. Gerry asked other Christians to pray about it. Tony appealed to Gerry's bosses. He won and found himself in a job just like his old one in a different branch of the company. He had a third heart attack. But he's still alive. Gerry did all he could to look after his employee's best interests, to put life before whatever it was that motivated Tony to risk it.

The boss's servant

Finally, Solomon has one more lesson for the Christian boss – three times in his prayer he calls himself God's 'servant'. Solomon has a keen sense that he gets his authority from God. That God made him king. That it is to God that he is ultimately accountable. Jesus, as we saw in chapter 10, makes the same point to Pilate – he would have no authority unless God had given it to him. This is a radical perspective. *God* has given you authority, not ultimately your company. And ultimately you are accountable to him. Certainly, your workplace may well have particular criteria for evaluating people's performance and potential, and they may have set aside certain funds for developing and training them but are they in line with God's criteria and development programme? Do you need to supplement them in some way? Do you need to work to have some of them changed?

As God's servant, as your people's servant, what's in their interests?

14

Moving in mysterious ways

Or you never can tell

'When the servant of the man of God got up
and went out early the next morning, an
army with horses and chariots had
surrounded the city. "Oh my lord, what
shall we do?" the servant asked.
"Don't be afraid," the prophet answered.
"Those who are with us are more than those
who are with them."
And Elisha prayed, "O Lord, open his eyes
so that he may see." Then the Lord opened
the servant's eyes, and he looked and saw the
hills full of horses and chariots of fire all
around Elisha.'

2 Kings 6: 14–17

• SNAPSHOTS •

1. Opportunity lost?

Let's call her Deborah. A wonderful person I'd been working with for over a year. She was Jewish, knew what I believed and had never raised the subject. Nor had I. It had never seemed right. We respected one another. I knew that I could have talked to her. And I knew that she would have listened. But I also felt that it would have been an abuse of our friendship. I would have been forcing something on her. So I never said anything overtly about the gospel. But I wanted her to hear it.

One day we were at a client's and due to travel back on the train together. I thought that there might be an opportunity to share something with Deborah. Towards the end of our meeting, our client said, 'Oh, are you travelling back by train? I'll come with you.'

'Aaagh! Nooooo! That's really blown it now,' I thought, but managed to feign delight. So we all toddled off to the train station together.

Five minutes into the train journey, completely out of the blue, with no preamble, no warning, no sidling cautiously up to the subject, the client, also Jewish, asked me why I believed what I believed.

So I told her.

After all, she was the client.

And of course Deborah was sitting right there with us. So she heard the gospel too.

I didn't have to engineer anything. I didn't have to manipulate a situation in which I could talk *at* her about Jesus, I didn't have to steer the conversation round to a religious topic. I didn't have to do anything.

God arranged it all.

2. Fourth time lucky?

Jim had failed his professional exams three times. And he wasn't putting money on himself to pass fourth time round. Tara was leaving the company but said to him, 'I'll pray for you.' She had developed the kind of relationship where she could say that kind of thing.

And she did pray.

Every day for a week until Jim's exams.

Four months later Tara went back to visit. Jim came running towards her like a long-lost lover in a romantic film. Or looking as romantic as you can running round a corner, weaving between the photocopier and the rubbish bin, and said, 'All those prayers worked. I passed.'

Others might be sceptical.

Jim himself had no doubts. Even though he was an avowed atheist, he knew, in this instance at least, where the bottom line was. And he wasn't worried about the apparent contradiction.

3. You never can tell

My boss had everything. A wonderful wife. Two lovely kids. Lots of friends. A great job with a great future and the respect and affection of those he worked for and those who worked for him. He also had a beautiful house. With a golf course across the road, and a ten handicap. This was a man without any needs. Except perhaps a little more accuracy with his fairway woods. I'd been praying for him.

One day we were going on a field trip together. Two men on a plane. Two men in a car. Two men wandering around a lot of supermarkets looking at cans and jars of coffee on shelves. Lunch with two other people. Two men in a car. Two men wandering around more supermarkets looking at cans and jars of coffee on shelves. It's all glamour in advertising.

We talked a lot. Actually, I tell a lie. Probably he talked a lot. And there's only so long you can talk about cans and jars of coffee. So we talked about pretty much everything else. All day we talked. Or probably he talked. I had prayed for an opportunity to talk about spiritual things. None came. Two men in a car. Then two men on a plane on a two hour flight back. He talked. We were almost there. And then the Captain comes on, 'Due to heavy traffic into La Guardia tonight we'll be up here a while longer. So sit back and relax and, as soon as we know, we'll let you know when we'll be touching down.'

He carried on talking. We carried on circling New York. I have to say I was getting a bit frustrated. There was absolutely no hint of an opening. I suppose I was altogether too focused on waiting for an opportunity to press my 'Here's the gospel' button rather than just enjoying the conversation and getting to know my boss better.

Anyway we circled. And he talked.

Half an hour passed. Then as he came to the end of describing a particular area of his life, I said, 'Well, it sounds like you've got everything pretty neatly tied up then?'

'Well,' he said, 'it's just this religion business that's bothering me at the moment.'

I didn't say much to that. He just talked about it for a while.

You never can tell what's going on with people, can you?